Twigs
In my
hair

Twigs In my hair

A Gardening Memoir

Cynthia Reyes

Photographs by Hamlin Grange

Published in 2019 by
Kingsgrange Books
Toronto

Hardcover Book ISBN 978-0-9918379-0-8
Paperback Book: ISBN: 978-0-9918379-2-2
Electronic Book: ISBN: 978-0-9918379-1-5

Cataloguing-in-Publication Data available from Library and Archives Canada

Photography: Hamlin Grange
Editors: Tim Knight and Donald Bastian
Writing Mentor: Lesley Marcovich
Cover & Book Design: Clif Graves
B & W illustration: Les Lawrence

Dedication

To Hamlin and our family, with love

Table of Contents
Introduction: Twigs in My Hair

LIVING WITH NATURE

GROWING WITH NATURE

Twigs in My Hair

Today I pretended it was normal to lie on the grass, face down, and weed. Dirt flew up my nose and there were twigs in my hair, but I kept going. Then I got up slowly and started toward the house; a patch of weeds waved at me like a red flag to a bull. So I sat in the garden bed, my back against a tree, and weeded.

Part 1
LIVING WITH NATURE

CHAPTER 1
A Child's Garden

More than half a century has passed, and yet each spring, when I wander into the primrose wood, I see the pale yellow blooms and smell their sweetest scent - for a moment I am seven years old again and wandering in that fragrant wood.

Gertrude Jekyll

My mother was a tender.

She tended the goats and chickens on our small farm in west central Jamaica. She tended the trees that bore oranges, lemons, breadfruit, and coconuts. Sometimes I heard her talking to them — the animals and trees — offering encouragement, waiting for a reply.

My mother had that way about her.

I think she was too busy tending to the animals, the trees, a husband, and a brood of five children — while also tending to her business designing and sewing dresses for neighbouring women — to stop and plant flowers.

Goodness knows all that tending was more than enough for even a woman as brave and strong as she. Perhaps she simply didn't have time to grow a flower garden.

Not then, anyway.

When I think of our little pink house in Jamaica today, I think of home and love and security and meals. And rules. Like be polite to your elders, wear clean underwear in case you're in an accident, and study so you won't be a disgrace to the family when you grow up.

Then I think of the tall grass and the trees and the stream that ran on one side of our property where there were no rules. It was our place of wildness and freedom. Our very own perfect children's garden.

It's where my sisters and I played hide-and-seek in the grass, climbed up and fell out of trees, splashed around in the stream.

Nature's own garden, I'd call it now. But those are the words of a grown woman. The child I was just called it home.

It wasn't until our family moved to our grandmother's much larger house in the village up the road that Mama tended her first flower garden. The garden was already there when we arrived but in need of care.

I remember it as a jewel box of pretty flowers. Red roses, yellow dahlias, orange zinnias and Joseph's Coat of Many Colours.

But I remember above everything else the Fairy Flowers. Clusters of them blooming in gentle colours. Pink, white, yellow, mauve. Unlike other flowers in the garden, these Fairy Flowers huddled close to the ground in small patches, as if looking after each other or keeping warm in the cool mountainside air.

Luminous, I'd call them now, because their petals seemed to glow. As if someone had tenderly polished each one till it shone. But these again are the words of an adult. As a child, all I knew was that I'd never seen anything so beautiful.

It was a mystery. The flowers would simply appear one day, as if a fairy had waved her magic wand. The tiny size of them and the magic of them made me decide that these were the flowers such beings grew in their own gardens. And once a year, they brought them as a present for us children.

But one day when I wasn't looking — perhaps when I was at school, or asleep in my bed at night — the Fairy Flowers just disappeared.

When that happened, I imagined that the fairies had taken them to another garden where other children would enjoy them. It was a sad and hopeful feeling all at once.

The timing of the flowers' arrival was always the same. Eastertime, or Holy Week, as churchgoing families called it. And so, surrounded by stories of Jesus' crucifixion and resurrection, my sisters and I decided we should show respect for the tiny pink, white, yellow, and mauve flowers. We'd call them Easter Lilies.

But every year when I saw them for the first time, I knew what they really were and who had left them for us.

It wasn't the first time — or the last — that I'd get my magic and miracles mixed up. My mind was always filled with wondrous thoughts and imaginings, especially during the pastor's long, boring sermons at church.

At church, at school, and especially at our dinner table, my sisters and I obeyed the rules and followed the beliefs of the adults around us. But when we were together, alone, we lived by the rules of our own world, complete with magical flowers.

As a grown woman and a gardener, I look back and wonder how such a small garden could harbour so many different kinds of flowers. But that's a question asked by an adult. The child in me knows the fairies and my mother worked together to create that garden.

And the child in me knows, without a shadow of a doubt, that it was my mother and the fairies who blessed me with my lifetime love of flowers.

"They need sunshine," Miss Catherine said. "Zinnias will grow anywhere if they have sunshine."

Miss Catherine was a friend of our family. Her garden was big and lush and dazzling, perhaps even more so to a small child. Flowers hung over her front fence in great bursts and splashes of colour. Yellows, pinks, reds, tangerines, and blues. People from all around stopped to admire them.

And now she had given me seeds from her flowers.

Hooray! my heart shouted. I would plant my own garden.

I decided that my garden was to be a secret. My secret. So I didn't ask my mother or anyone else for help.

When no one was looking, I borrowed the oldest-looking silver fork from my mother's cabinet drawer. I imagined it as my magic wand.

I found a patch of red Jamaican earth where the sun shone all day and nothing was growing and dug into it with my wand. Then I scattered Miss Catherine's zinnia seeds, covered them with a thin layer of soil, and patted the soil down.

In my mind I could already see the pretty pink, red, and orange flowers that would grow from those seeds. I could hardly wait for my family to see them, too. What a great surprise that would be!

I checked my garden before and after school every day. On Saturdays when there was no school and on Sundays after church, I checked it every hour, bending down so close to the earth that my nose touched.

I watched and waited till my excitement grew so big I thought my heart would burst right through my chest.

The weeks went by. Nothing happened. No green shoots broke through the soil. No flowers bloomed. No garden grew.

Had I asked my mother, she would have told me I hadn't "put two and two together."

Because there was a reason why nothing ever grew in that soil. The earth had been parched by the broiling Jamaican sun over the years, baked dry of all its nutrients. And when the rain fell on it, it ran right off its iron-hard surface.

That was my first garden. And it almost broke my heart.

In our front yard, in the shelter of the house's walls and a flowering tree fed daily by glorious Jamaican sunshine, Mama's small jewel-box garden flourished. She tended it mostly in the early mornings, right after she gave us all breakfast.

Roses and dahlias and zinnias and Joseph's Coat of Many Colours.

And once a year, of course, my Fairy Flowers.

It was then I knew that when I became an adult and had my own home, I would have a garden, too. Just like Mama. I would plant flowers in rich soil. Roses, dahlias, zinnias, and the strangely named Joseph's Coat of Many Colours.

And perhaps one day the fairies would bring me a gift of tiny flowers in pink, white, yellow, and mauve.

And, just like Mama, I would have my own magical jewel-box garden.

One day.

CHAPTER 2
A Garden of Our Own

However many years she lived, Mary always felt that she should never forget that first morning when her garden began to grow.

Frances Hodgson Burnett, The Secret Garden

At last.

It finally happened, decades later. I was all grown up and living in Toronto, Canada, with my husband, Hamlin, and our young daughter, Nikisha.

Hamlin and I both had good jobs as journalists — he, with Canada's largest newspaper, The Toronto Star; I, with Canada's largest broadcaster, the Canadian Broadcasting Corporation. We decided that it was time to buy a home of our own.

After much looking around, falling in love with entirely inappropriate homes, and being talked out of them by Harry, our very sensible realtor, we finally bought a narrow, two-storey, red-brick house in the east end of Toronto.

Its best features were that it was affordable and in good shape. A "solid and sensible" house, Harry called it. Its second-best feature was the long, narrow patch of land behind the house. It faced east, south, and west, which even a beginner like me knew was a good thing. It would get "good sun."

Hooray! I'd finally have my own garden.

My garden yearning was so strong that it reached out and infected my husband. Before we knew it, we were planning our garden together. During late evenings that winter, after we'd put our young daughter to bed, Hamlin and I pulled out a large sheet of paper and worked on the first drawings.

"What do you think of a garden bed here, another over there, and railway ties to separate them?" Hamlin asked across our small wooden kitchen table.

I nodded eager agreement as his fingers flew across the paper.

It was bliss. We agreed on everything and returned to our separate dreams. Husband dreamed of tomatoes, green lettuce, and corn. Wife dreamed of yellow nasturtiums, red dahlias, and pink roses. And as many couples do, we forgot to share the details.

The winter slowly withdrew, helped on its way by the arrival of gentle rains and milder temperatures. The first birds sang. The first tulip I planted the autumn we moved in poked its head out of the soil in a corner of the front yard. I had never seen a bulb I'd planted emerge the next spring.

It was a miracle. I ran back inside the house, shrieking in delight.

"Come see! Come see!" I called out and pulled my fellow gardener out to see the miracle. He still wore his robe and pajamas, had his coffee mug in hand.

"This is what you dragged me out of the house so early in the morning to see?" he asked, staring at the miracle first, then at me. Indeed, it was just after six a.m. "A tulip popping out of the ground?"

I was practically jumping up and down and rocking on my heels. I didn't catch the note of skepticism. But then I saw him shrug.

How could I explain that he was looking at a genuine miracle? That this was the first time something I planted had come to life? That this miracle plant reminded me of the fairy flowers of my early childhood, the little jewels that showed up only once a year at Easter?

But Hamlin, who had grown up in Canada and had seen spring bulbs come to life every year, wasn't impressed.

It was a sign of things to come. But I was too excited to notice.

A few weeks later, I was upstairs in the bathroom brushing my teeth when a male voice cried out, "Attaboy! You finally did it!"

I ran down the stairs, toothbrush still in hand.

Hamlin stood at the kitchen window. He was leaning over a huge flower pot with a smile of pure joy on his face. "They did it. They finally did it!"

I had no idea what was happening. "Who did what?"

"The peas!" Hamlin yelled, pointing at the flowerpot, with a look that said *Are you blind, or what?*

I leaned over. I could barely make out little dots of green poking their heads from the soil. "Hmmm …" I tried really hard to sound enthusiastic. "Aha …"

Three-year-old Nikisha had heard her father's shouts and came running down from her bedroom. Hamlin pointed out the tiny green dots and told her what they were, and her eyes lit up with the wonder of a child seeing magic.

As I climbed the stairs to complete the task of brushing my teeth, I thought, Strange how Hamlin had mocked my miracle yet been so excited by his own.

But I still didn't realize that we were headed for a conflict of horticultural proportions.

Soon, our garden drawings came alive. The soil was worked, beds marked, dividers put in place. It was only a week to the May 24 holiday weekend when people in Toronto plant their gardens, hoping there's no more danger of a killer frost.

I could see our garden in my mind. One, maybe two beds for Hamlin's vegetables, and the rest nothing but beautiful flowers. Lilies, gladioli, sweet alyssum, nasturtium ... mmm. I could practically smell them.

A friend gave me our first gift for the garden — peony plants that bloom big, rose-like pink flowers. Fragrant flowers. I planted them in the largest garden bed. With that simple act, our garden was born.

It was time to rejoice.

A few hours later, a madman confronted me in the kitchen.

"Did you plant flowers in my bed?" he roared. Yes, my beloved husband, normally so calm and polite, roared at me.

I forced myself to answer calmly. "Oh, you mean the peonies? Sure. I planted a few in the large bed on the right. It gets the best sun."

"But that's the bed I plan to put tomatoes in!" he half-snarled, half-wailed. "I spent hours preparing that bed!"

I tried to think up a reasonable solution. He didn't wait for it.

"I don't want any flowers in that part of the garden," he declared. "Plant them somewhere else!"

I told myself, I must remember that this man loves me. He's shown it in countless ways. But the kind, sensible, decent man I had fallen in love with years earlier had disappeared. And this stranger in front of me had just declared war.

"What do you mean?" I shouted. "This house belongs to both of us. Same goes for the garden. You can't tell me where to plant my flowers!"

Hamlin hesitated for just a moment, and his voice, when it came, was too measured, too calm.

"Can you eat flowers?" he asked.

It was a low blow.

A long and angry silence hung in the air.

My fellow gardener took a deep breath. "Listen," he said, trying to soothe me. "I'll dig some beds closer to the back of the house. That area also gets good sun and you can plant your flowers there."

"But the earth there isn't as rich as the soil in those other beds."

"It is, it is. That's where some of your spring bulbs are now, and they're doing well, aren't they?"

Reluctantly, I admitted this was true.

That Saturday, we visited the garden centre together. Hamlin headed straight for the edible seedlings, the little green plants that would grow up and become vegetables. I headed for the inedibles, the little green plants that would grow up to bloom beautiful, colourful, fragrant flowers.

He went for romaine lettuces. I decided to try gladiolus bulbs. He reached for a packet of basil seeds. I reached for a packet of cleome seeds.

We paid for our choices separately and met again in the doorway.

"What's all that?" we each asked. At exactly the same time.

Before he could answer, I was overcome by the urge to challenge. "Why on earth are you buying romaine lettuce? We rarely ever eat the stuff!"

"The same reason you're buying ..." he reached over and pulled a packet of cleome seeds from my black plastic garden centre tray, "... clomies."

Clomies, he'd called them!

We stared at each other, moved out of the way to let other shoppers pass, then started laughing at the absurdity of it all.

"Come on," I said softly. "Flowers are good for the spirit."

Hamlin didn't have to say it, but I knew what he was thinking: Flowers are good for the spirit, but vegetables are good for the stomach.

Slowly we learned to garden together. Compromising here, giving way there, throwing a fit now and then, always making up in the end.

As the weeks went by, I had to admit that his rows of vegetables and herbs looked surprisingly healthy, and at harvest time were entirely edible.

And one warm day in early summer he finally admitted that the beauty of my flowers did something good for his soul.

Through our garden, we were learning to live together, solve problems together, build a strong foundation for our marriage. Our garden was the place where we grew up.

It was also the place where Nikisha planted her first garden. She sowed carrot seeds in a half-barrel, and they grew and tasted of bliss.

And then one day — hooray — our second daughter, Lauren, came along.

The garden became a happy place for all four of us, as well as relatives and friends who visited and Barclay, the dog who joined our family. Yes, he had a habit of eating green tomatoes right off the vine. But that seemed a small price to pay for all the joy our garden gave him and us.

CHAPTER 3
Lessons from a Master

A garden is a grand teacher. It teaches patience and careful watchfulness; it teaches industry and thrift; above all it teaches entire trust.

Gertrude Jekyll

Mr. Smith lived in an old house on a double lot on a side street in Toronto. I remember the first time I glimpsed his garden. It was a Saturday afternoon in mid-summer, and I was driving past his home. I did a double-take, hit the brakes, reversed, stopped the car, and got out so I could see more.

A tall, angular, white-haired man was deadheading some roses. He wore spectacles, was neatly dressed in a white shirt and dress trousers as if he was heading for some important meeting. He didn't look like any gardener I'd ever seen before.

Even so, I knew that this was his garden, and he was the gardener. I could see it in how he bent over to study his flowers and the soil around them the way an artist studies his unfinished painting on canvas.

I walked up and bravely said hello.

He looked up and gave a shy little half-laugh. "Hello."

Something about that laugh endeared him to me, along with his grandfatherly age and look. I had never known either of my grandfathers because both died before I was born.

His flowers were everywhere. Running their riotous ways around the house and into the distance of his back garden, becoming more muted in the soft shade of trees, then re-emerging in all their glory in the brilliant sunlit spaces. Big, fat dahlias, snapdragons, and roses jostled for space with a multitude of other brilliantly coloured flowers.

The garden was heaven on earth.

I finally noticed the house, too. It was long and thin, while the garden was fat and wide. It seemed to me to be a garden with a house attached, not the other way around.

I visited Mr. Smith occasionally that summer and again during the following growing season. And so it continued for a few years. This gentle man never seemed to tire of my pesky questions and never once said what he probably should have: "Why don't you go buy a gardening book and stop bothering me?"

Every time I stopped to admire his garden, and sometimes when I asked him the name of a particular flower, he answered patiently and then gave me a new plant for my own fledgling garden.

He was intrigued by the strange names I used to identify some of the flowers in his garden as I flitted about pointing at flower after flower.

One day I stopped before a plant whose large, textured, multicoloured leaves I recognized immediately. "Oh, look at this. Joseph's Coat. My mother had that in her garden in Jamaica. It grew year-round. But I had no idea it would grow in Canada as well."

"It's an annual here." He was tying a tall, top-heavy blue delphinium to a thin bamboo stake. "It only grows here in the warm months. But what's that name you called it?"

"Joseph's Coat. From the Bible story about Joseph's coat of many colours. What do you call it? Does it have another name?"

"Coleus," he said.

I thought Joseph's Coat was a much better name but didn't tell Mr. Smith.

We strolled together towards a plant stand behind the house where annual and perennial flowers in pots waited to be planted. Mr. Smith picked up one of the pots and handed it to me. The label said "Coleus" but I knew it was really Joseph's Coat.

"For you," he said. I accepted it gratefully, held onto it like a prize.

Mr. Smith started most of his annual flowers from seeds or cuttings taken from mature plants in his own garden. When winter loomed, the weather grew cold, and his garden had been put to bed, he worked with his indoor plants. House windowsills were his conservatory.

He started a new African violet, geranium, or coleus from a single leaf or shoot in water inside a plastic cup. When it sprouted roots, he tucked it into a small green plastic pot, two-thirds filled with moist potting soil.

One day he handed me a pot as I left for home. "Keep the soil moist for a while."

"What's 'a while'?"

It was either my brashness or his shyness that made him laugh — that same gentle half-laugh he made whenever I confronted him with one of my ignorant questions about how to get things to grow.

"Oh, maybe a week or so," he replied, with the assurance of the experienced gardener.

"Or so?" I asked, smiling back at him with the ignorance of the novice.

"When it starts to grow or send out another shoot, you should ease up and then only water it when the soil gets dry. If you overwater it, the plant might develop a fungus or shrivel up where the stem meets the soil."

I pretended to be a quick study in horticultural matters. "Okay, thanks!"

Every time I left Mr. Smith's house with my prize of tiny plants in little plastic pots, I hoped desperately that I wouldn't screw up his directions. I didn't want to disappoint him with the news that some plant he'd so tenderly started and entrusted to my care had died. I couldn't imagine ever lying to this lovely, grandfatherly man.

Late summer in Mr. Smith's garden meant it was time for him to collect seeds from the annual flowers. Some he started growing in late winter in a flat plastic tray on a windowsill. Some he would scatter on the earth in the spring.

He gave me tiny envelopes containing seeds from each of these flowers and instructions on how and when to plant them.

Among them were my favourites. Delicate pink California poppies and cosmos, the daisy-shaped flower with silky petals that grew in white or pink. Snow-on-the-mountain, whose variegated green and white leaves were crowned by bracts of tiny white flowers.

In the early years of my gardening lessons, Mr. Smith had to be patient. "You can take a chance and sprinkle some seeds on the bed in the fall and maybe they'll sprout in the late spring," he'd tell me. "But remember, they're annuals, not used to Canada's cold winters. Some seeds should only be planted in May, once the frost has passed."

In time I learned to recognize — even understand — Mr. Smith's instructions. Even so, whether I planted in fall or spring, my seeds never seemed to sprout and grow into the big, beautiful flowers that made Mr. Smith's garden so glorious.

One late summer, Hamlin and I decided that a flowering shrub would look really great in our front garden, so I went to my gardening guru for advice.

We were standing side by side in his garden eyeing a shade-loving Joseph's Coat whose dark red foliage had mysteriously shrivelled up. "Mr. Smith …" I started.

He squinted sideways at me, waiting for my newest silly question.

"I need to plant a flowering shrub in my front garden. What should I plant?"

"We-e-ellll …" he said, then fell silent.

I imagined he was trying to think of something even a witless neophyte like me couldn't kill.

"Now's actually a good time to plant shrubs," he said. "How about a forsythia?"

"A forsythia …" I tried to pretend I knew what he was talking about. "What colour are the blooms again?"

"Yellow."

"Right … of course … yellow."

"As long as it gets sunlight, it will bloom. Needs a bit of pruning after it blooms, but some go for years without pruning."

"Where's the best place to buy a … forsythia?" I asked.

He named a nearby plant nursery. "It usually has healthy trees and shrubs. Costs a bit more than other places but worth it. I'm going there next week. I could buy one for you, and we can settle up later."

I was at home writing when the doorbell rang. It was Mr. Smith, toting a healthy-looking shrub of some sort.

"Here's the forsythia," he announced proudly. "Where do you want to plant it?"

"Right there in the middle of the garden in the front."

He carried the shrub nestled in his arm, laid it gently on the grass. Then he went back to his car and fetched a spade, a rake, and a couple of trowels. Less than an hour later, the forsythia was planted, watered, and much admired by both of us. I refunded Mr. Smith the price. It was the only time that money ever changed hands between us.

Mr. Smith kept giving me flowers and plants and, along the way, gardening lessons that were as much a delight as planting seedlings.

One hot summer day I estimated the cost of the many plants he had given me during our two gardening seasons. It came to hundreds of dollars. I suddenly felt I was taking advantage of this kind old man.

So I mustered a reasoned mathematical argument about what it would have cost me to buy the plants in a nursery and handed Mr. Smith an envelope containing several twenty-dollar bills the next time I saw him.

"I need to do this, please …" I told him shyly.

He opened the envelope. I could see hurt in his eyes. He just stood there holding the envelope in his hand like he didn't know what it was.

I tried to explain. "Mr. Smith," I said. "I hate when people take advantage of others, especially people who are …"

I frantically tried to find another word for old. "… elderly," I finished lamely.

He just stared at me, then he handed back the envelope.

I tried to recover. "You know, Mr. Smith … I'm a young woman and you're an … elderly man … and I don't want to take advantage … it's a matter of not taking advantage … and … I guess it's pride, too, Mr. Smith. But I don't mean to be rude. I'm sorry ..."

I meant everything I said. But everything I said was wrong.

After a moment's silence, I picked up a trowel, walked to a nearby flower-bed, and started weeding. Mr. Smith grabbed a garden fork and turned over the soil in a bed where he planned to put some plants that were doing poorly under the shade of a tree.

We continued gardening — standing, bending, kneeling, pottering around within easy talking distance of each other — but never talking. Once, absorbed in our tasks, we nearly collided with each other. We laughed but still didn't speak.

We carried on like this, the silence growing more and more companionable, until somewhere along the way it occurred to me that we were talking again — talking through the soil, through the plants, through our love for gardening.

It was only later that I realized why Mr. Smith had been so hurt.

He was in his eighties. He'd raised four children on his own after his wife died, and in the decades since they'd grown up and left home, he'd lived by himself. He cooked, cleaned, and gardened by himself, read newspapers and books by himself, ate his meals by himself.

He had never once asked me to help him in any way. Not even to do an errand on the way to his home, which I could easily have done. His was a truly independent spirit.

He'd given me a priceless gift by allowing me to invade his space and gradually become a gardening friend. Perhaps he sensed that, as an independent spirit myself, I would understand and respect his need for dignity, especially as he got older.

But I had been blinded by my need to not be indebted. And my efforts to preserve my own pride had ended up wounding his. I didn't know what to do to remove the hurt I had caused this sweet and gentle man.

One afternoon Mr. Smith invited me into his kitchen for a cold drink. We sat at the small kitchen table, and I told him how nicely his garden was doing. He claimed that it was a mess and needed more tending.

"Mr. Smith," I said. "How on earth can you say such a thing? Your garden is incredibly beautiful!"

"Oh, no," he replied, with his small, modest laugh. "It's not as nice as some others I've seen."

"It's way nicer than any other garden for miles around!"

"Ah," he said, the look on his face indicating that it was nice of me to say so, but his was, all the same, just a humble, messy little garden.

"I'd give a lot to have a garden half as beautiful and lush and healthy as this one," I said. "It would take me forever, though. How on earth do you get it to look like this?" I peered through the back window and gestured to the garden.

He laughed that humble laugh again, and even seemed to blush. "You just said the word. It's all in mother earth. It's all in the soil. Everything starts with good soil."

This was true. I'd watched him take hours to prepare the soil in a bed. A mix of compost, topsoil, and moistened peat moss was his favourite. His soil was naturally sandy; the peat moss, compost and topsoil provided texture and nutrients to it.

When he had mixed the soil exactly as he wanted, he made a hole and placed the plant gently into it, making sure to spread out the roots to stop them from becoming root-bound. Only then did he fill the space around the plant stem with soil, carefully tamp it down, and sprinkle it with water.

Finally, of course, like every gardener who's ever lived, he'd step back and admire.

Mr. Smith firmly believed in buying healthy, vigorous plants even if they were more expensive. And when it came to annuals like impatiens or geraniums he always bought plants with still-closed blooms.

"Everyone wants to get instant blooms," he'd say. "But you shouldn't buy a plant that's too advanced. Let it get over the transplant shock and get used to its spot in the garden while it's still young. Bigger plants, and plants with blooms, have a tougher time making it through the transplant."

He believed in buying sturdy, but not large, shrubs, knowing that they too would make a better transition from pot to garden if transplanted young.

I learned a lot from Mr. Smith. I watched him patiently, carefully prepare soil, make sure roots were healthy and able to spread, and choose places where plants could flourish and grow. But most of all I learned to start small and let my plants grow at their own pace.

These were important lessons for a stubborn, impatient young woman who wanted a beautiful garden and wanted it now.

Only later would I realize these were also important lessons for life.

Mr. Smith and I never discussed money again. On the matter of my guilty conscience over the plants I took from his garden, we finally came to an unspoken agreement. He gave me plants and allowed me to help him in the garden and, once in a while, give him small presents. A utensil for his kitchen, perhaps. Or a tool for his garden.

It was a compromise between two independent souls. He was never really comfortable accepting my gifts, and I was never really comfortable accepting so many plants from his garden. But we were both sensible enough to realize we had a good garden friendship and each of us needed to compromise a little.

With that hurdle overcome, our relationship mellowed.

As the years passed, I started travelling for my demanding job in network television. Also, I had a husband, two beautiful young daughters, and a shared dog. So gardening was my way of keeping sane in the midst of heavy demands on my time and energy. But it also meant I didn't see Mr. Smith as often.

One day I came back from a trip to Vancouver and called Mr. Smith about some problems with my roses. I hadn't seen him for about three months. He didn't answer the phone. I tried again later. And again the next day.

I went around to his house. No answer to my knocking.

I phoned his daughter. She told me he'd had a stroke and when he was released from hospital had been moved into her home. I asked about his condition. It wasn't good.

"I need to see him, please. Do you think I could visit?"

"He's not been accepting visitors," she said. "But I know how fond he is of you, Cynthia. I'll see if he'll change his mind."

The following day she called to tell me her father hadn't changed his mind. The news shocked me into silence. His daughter tried to explain.

"You know how independent he is, Cynthia," she said. "He did everything for himself, in spite of his age. And he was proud of it. He just doesn't want you to see him in this condition now."

My brain understood, but not my heart.

I thought back to the day when I tried to pay him for his flowers. Dignity was truly important to Mr. Smith then and even more important now.

I never saw Mr. Smith again.

When he died I was working in South Africa, the land of the protea, the arum lily, the bird-of-paradise, and the agapanthus. Home to some of the world's most popular flowers.

It was impossible to look at such beauty without remembering my gardening teacher — the tall, angular, white-haired, gentle man with the shy half-laugh who'd taught me a whole lot about life while helping me make things grow.

CHAPTER 4
Patience, Young Friend

True obedience:
silently the flowers speak
to the inner ear

Onitsura

C anada had been good to me. I had arrived here in the early 70's, attended university while holding down a full-time job, and was recruited by CBC Television News even before graduation.

By my early thirties, I was that rare thing in network television: a young, Black, immigrant woman who was also an executive producer and a rising star. As far as I knew, I was the only one of my kind anywhere in the country.

I had developed a reputation for being talented, visionary, fearless. I thrived on tough challenges and hired people who shared a similar attitude.

All those privileges meant I had the skills and influence to help others, as Hamlin occasionally reminded me. And, from time to time, a biblical saying rang in my ears: "For unto whomsoever much is given, of him shall be much required".

I became a community volunteer. It was as a board member, then president of the Black Business and Professional Association (BBPA), that my path crossed with Donald Moore's.

In 1984, the BBPA presented Mr. Moore with an award for his leading role in changing Canada's immigration laws thirty years before.

In 1954, Canada's immigration policy still had a "colour bar" in place; Black and Asian immigrants from Commonwealth countries were not welcome.

Born in Barbados, Donald Moore was one of very few Caribbean immigrants allowed into the country in the early 1900's. He came by way of the United States. In Canada, he worked as a train porter. He saved and studied. A brilliant student, he was accepted into the dentistry program at Nova Scotia's Dalhousie University in 1918.

A lengthy illness ended his dream of becoming a dentist; he became a tailor and dry cleaner instead, soon operating his own business. He was also a community leader. He founded the Negro Citizenship Association, a humanitarian and social organization.

On Tuesday, April 27, 1954, Donald Moore led a delegation of community and church leaders, veterans, and trade unionists to Ottawa. They convinced the Canadian government to change the law.

Mr. Moore had changed the course of Canadian history. But until the BBPA honoured him in 1984, relatively few people knew what he had done. I was one of them: I didn't know that I, and others like me, owed Mr. Moore a tremendous debt.

In 1986, I decided it was time to nominate him and his contemporary, Harry Gairey, for Canada's highest honour, the Order of Canada.

It was time. It was the right thing to do. I was now the president of the BBPA and, compared to the challenges I took on at work, this one seemed small.

One of Donald Moore's best investments was made decades before I met him at his home on a side street in north Toronto. In 1942, he and a small group of other Black Canadians had purchased two-acre lots on what seemed, at the time, more country lane than city street.

Now retired, he still lived there with his wife, Kay.

Mr. Moore was working in his greenhouse when I arrived to interview him. It was attached to the house, a small room with glass walls and ceiling, and dozens of plants on benches and shelves.

"Don!" his wife called, drawing his attention to the visitor. He turned toward me, a tall, trim man wearing glasses, his long fingers holding a small pot with something green growing in it. He promptly put it down, turned away from his plant cuttings of varying sizes, wiped his hands, and came to greet me.

Mr. Moore had keen eyes and a dignified manner. He was the kind of person you immediately looked up to, and not only because of his height.

In that meeting and the ones that followed, I marvelled at his eloquence and knowledge, and his fine recall of events long past.

I visited him several times, and almost every time, I would find Mr. Moore tending his plants in the greenhouse. His hands held a pot or a trowel, a clipper or a watering can, his fingers moved nimbly between green leaves or poked into the soil.

"I think you must live in that greenhouse, Mr. Moore!" I teased one day as we greeted each other.

Each time, before I left, our talk turned to his flowers, and we would transform almost instantly from interviewer and interviewee to avid gardeners. These were happy talks, educational talks.

Mr. Moore's spacious and lush perennial garden had won horticultural awards, with good reason. He tended it lovingly. When spring came, I was eager to see it, and he was happy to show me around.

We strolled along paths and across the lawn. Mr. Moore and I frequently stopped to look at a flower I'd never seen before.

"And what's that one called?" I asked often, pointing and waiting for him to answer. I was like a small child in a candy store. I might as well have been hopping from foot to foot in excitement.

As we started back toward the house, I noticed several black plastic pots in which tiny seedlings grew. I stopped Mr. Moore yet again.

"What are you growing in those pots, Mr. Moore?" I asked, pointing.

"Trees," he answered. "Maples."

"But... but it'll be decades before they get big," I said.

"Yes," he said.

"Why bother?" I asked.

"All trees were small like this once," he said, eyes smiling down at me.

"Yes," I said. "But..."

But he was 94. But he couldn't live much longer.

I couldn't bring myself to say it out loud, but Mr. Moore was no such coward.

"I won't be around to see them mature," he completed my thought. "But someone else will."

I fell quiet, embarrassed. But there was no need, I quickly realized. Mr. Moore was smiling at me without any hint of judgment. I felt like a child who had just learned an important lesson from a caring elder.

I loved him for it.

I did not have a large garden and so could not take one of the tiny trees home with me. Mr. Moore, instead, gave me a small evergreen boxwood plant, about as big as my index finger.

I looked up at him and grinned, wondering aloud how many years it would take to become a real shrub.

"All you need is patience," he said. And all the plant needed was a bit of watering to get it established and a place in the sun to grow.

I took the boxwood from his hands, receiving it as reverently as a worshipper at church would receive the sacramental bread and wine.

The boxwood plant found its place in a sunny spot of our garden. When we moved from our first house, it was dug up and relocated along with us. Every time I spied it in our garden, I thought of Mr. Moore and his lesson about patience.

I, meanwhile, was trying – oh, how I tried to learn patience. But life had tests in store.

Years earlier, I had learned this lesson well: never try to pay a gardener for plants you've been freely given. A small gift, however, is perfectly acceptable.

One day, as a token of our friendship, I brought Mr. Moore a pink azalea. Some azaleas are hardy, surviving Canada's cold winters and putting out new flowers each spring. But I bought this one in a supermarket and learned from the tag that it was not recommended for outdoor planting.

On a later visit a year or so later, Mr. Moore was again in his greenhouse when I arrived. Smiling mysteriously, he beckoned me to come closer.

"Remember this?" His long, slender fingers hugged a potted plant. The plant was full of blooms. Pink blooms.

"Is that… that can't be… is that the azalea I gave you, Mr. Moore?"

"It is!" he said, smiling proudly.

He had tended it carefully, pruning, watering and fertilizing, and here it was now, with a profusion of blooms.

It became a ritual: on every visit, I would step into the greenhouse to check up on the azalea, and Mr. Moore always smiled when I re-emerged.

Our friendship developed and bloomed along with the azalea.

After one visit, I tried to puzzle it out in my journal:

> *My dearest gardening friends are decades older than me. Some, like Mr. Smith, I'd met through their gardens. Others, like Mr. Moore, I'd met in different circumstances, then discovered they were gardeners.*
>
> *However we met, we became good friends.*
>
> *Why is that?*

Is it because they're long retired, allowing them time to garden and to develop a relationship with a young person who clearly wants to learn?

But why did I grow to care so deeply for them? Was it because immigration separated me from the elderly members of my own family? Am I trying to find substitute grandfathers?

I had never even seen a photo of my grandfathers; both died before I was born. My maternal grandfather had been an inventor and a jeweler, and I always imagined him as being a tall, thin man with nimble fingers, but I didn't know that for sure. I didn't even know if either grandfather liked flowers, or liked to plant things.

No, I wrote. Mr. Smith and Mr. Moore are both elderly, tall and thin, but they won me over on their own merits, particularly their love of gardening.

And anyway, I speculated to my journal, maybe the answers are both simpler and more profound at the same time.

Gardening touches something elemental within the gardener. The airs and pretenses we put on in the workplace or at social events don't stand a chance when you're kneeling on the ground, sweat rolling from your forehead, all ten fingers grimy, dirt on your cheeks and twigs in your hair.

There's an old Greek proverb that says: "A society grows great when old men plant trees whose shade they know they shall never sit in."

Mr. Moore had lived quietly at his home in North Toronto, neither expecting nor soliciting recognition for his contributions to Canada. Contributions that had provided 'shade' for my generation of immigrants.

My BBPA colleague, Tessa Benn-Ireland, and I worked on the two nominations together and submitted them, hoping both Mr. Moore and Mr. Gairey would be honoured at the same time. Both had done so much for our country.

Mr. Gairey, the younger of the two but better known, was inducted into the Order of Canada that year.

Mr. Moore wasn't chosen that year. Or the next. Or the next.

Year after year, I nominated him, my patience growing even thinner as time passed. Sometimes, embarrassed by my failure, months would pass before I visited Mr. Moore again.

I had been successful at almost every challenge I had undertaken. Why on earth was I failing at this? Perhaps equally important: why was I taking it so personally?

I knew the answer to that latter question, of course. I was hurt on Mr. Moore's behalf. He deserved this honour. And, as his friend, I watched him getting older, frailer.

It would be four years before the nomination was successful. In 1990, just a few years before his death at the age of 102, Mr. Moore was inducted into the Order of Canada.

The long wait and many submissions had challenged both my patience and maturity. When I got the news, my eyes filled with tears. It had happened, at last.

However he felt inside, Mr. Moore seemed calm about the big news. He had, after all, waited decades to be honoured by his own community for the bold changes he had led decades earlier.

And, as I wrote in my journal years later: This was, after all, a man who, in his late nineties, still started trees from seeds.

CHAPTER 5
Guilty Pleasures

*Beware the all-consuming passion. But even more, beware the
passionless life.*

From My Journal

It all started so innocently. In the dead of winter. The sort of drab, colourless,
endlessly cold Canadian winter that drives some people to drink.

But what's a non-drinker to do?

What I did, when the whole world felt like a frozen wasteland and I was
truly at my lowest, was buy my first magazine.

And so it was that I began my days and nights of sin. I became a dirty old
woman. The female version of the man who hides certain magazines between
the mattress and the box spring.

And so it was that in airports, train stations, and bookstores, I hovered in
front of magazine racks, found the one most likely to slake my thirst, opened it
—and there they were. Inviting. Beautiful. Complete with luscious centrefolds.

I lusted.

My heart would beat faster. Break into a little sweat. I glanced around.
When no one was looking, I headed to the cashier, magazine carefully rolled so
the front cover was hidden.

If I was with a friend or business colleague, I also bought camouflage — one
of those serious magazines with cover stories like "Whither Canada?"

The camouflage was supposed to hide the prize but usually didn't. If anyone asked, I insisted that I buy the magazine for the stories. And then I did my best to keep a straight face.

"Pornography for us older folk," my friend Les once called my passion. I giggled nervously, muttered that I was just browsing, certainly not an addict.

But I knew of what he spoke. Oh, how well did I know.

Back home, afraid of my husband's scorn ("Another of those magazines?"), I hid the magazine under my blouse and headed to the bathroom. In the tub, once in the steaming hot water and bubbled up to my chin, I gave in to my yearning for all things beautiful yet unattainable.

Unable, unwilling, to resist any longer.

I open the magazine. And I am transported to the lavish land of fantasy. I drown in its beauty.

Behold the splendour. The undulating curves. The hills, valleys, beds and passions of my shameful desire. Unimaginable, untouchable beauties of every shape and colour. Many from hot, exotic places where palm trees sway. The Caribbean, Japan, Thailand.

I inhale deeply, breathing in their heady perfume. I'm intoxicated, swept away by their beauty.

It's a drug. One magazine is one too many, and a thousand are not enough.

I've tried to break the addiction. Once I even locked a pile of the magazines in a box and put the box in the garage under a pile of old shelving, praying, No more. Never again. Get thee behind me, Satan.

But the path to damnation is littered with good intentions. As I endure this awful Canadian winter — the endless days of shortened sunlight or none at all, trapped indoors for months at a time — my good intentions fall by the wayside.

I've tried. Lord knows, I've tried.

But I'm weak.

So off I go to buy another gardening magazine.

CHAPTER 6
A Patch of Purple Iris

The kiss of the sun for pardon,
The song of the birds for mirth,
One is nearer God's Heart in a garden
Than anywhere else on earth.

Dorothy Frances Gurney 'God's Garden'

Falling in love with a patch of purple flowers in someone else's garden can be as dangerous as falling in love with a stranger.

You tell yourself at the time that, at worst, it will be exciting, maybe even fun. That, in the end, no real harm will be done. Then, in retrospect, you realize that you got much more than you bargained for.

But let me start at the beginning.

In the past, I had a simple way of getting the horticultural objects of my desire from strangers — I bought them. It always followed the same pattern. I'd approach the gardener politely and talk gardening for a while.

All gardeners love to talk gardening. It's one of the rules of the craft. Then I'd mention a particular flower or shrub in the garden, admire it, and offer a fair price.

Money and plants would change hands. Never once had I been turned down.

But there's always a first time.

One lovely spring day, while Hamlin and I were driving home from an errand, I noticed a woman on her knees weeding around a prominent patch of something purple. It looked a lot like a particularly vivid iris. Of course, I asked Hamlin to stop the car so I could get a closer look.

This was not the time for procuring flowers. Our family was between gardens, or homes, I should say. We had accepted an offer on our current home but were still a few months away from moving into the next. Swept away by the beauty of the tall purple irises, however, I immediately forgot that minor detail.

The woman, somewhere in her late sixties, graciously returned my greeting as if strangers interrupted her gardening every day.We talked the mandatory gardening talk for a while, and then, after I'd seen the flowers close up, I got right down to business.

"I really love those purple irises," I told her.

Pushing my luck, I declared that the flowers had obviously outgrown their bed. "So, I wonder if when you're dividing them, I could buy some from you. We'll be moving into a new house soon and will be happy to pay …"

She smiled broadly. Most gardeners love people admiring their flowers, and this woman was obviously no different.

"I'll be happy to give you some," she said. "But I won't sell them."

Any sensible person would have accepted gladly, refusing to look a gift horse in the mouth (one of my mother's favourite sayings). Certainly any sensible person who remembered the lesson learned from offering dear Mr. Smith money for his flowers would have graciously accepted.

But not me. Good sense had flown the coop.

I heard myself announcing primly, and for all the wrong reasons: "I simply can't do that. It wouldn't be right. We don't even know each other."

Even as I said the words, I regretted them.

The-woman-who-would-not-sell-her-irises changed the subject. "Would you like to see the rest of the garden?"

"That would be just wonderful! But my husband's waiting in the car."

"He's welcome, too."

Hamlin and I followed her down the garden path between the main house and a small stone cottage. Then we turned the corner.

Before us, within the ruins of what looked like an overgrown mini-Stonehenge, was an abundance – no, a riot -- of blooming flowers. The sweet fragrance of massed flowers perfumed the spring air and held us spellbound.

Our host told us these ruined half-walls of stone had once been stables.

Each now sheltered its own small garden.

White-flowered climbing hydrangea and fragrant yellow sweet alyssum tumbled and sprawled along the broken walls, exuberantly ignoring any suggestion of containment.

Hamlin and I repeatedly glanced at each other, eyes open wide in delight and surprise.

In one stall, smothered in large, delicate pink flowers, was the largest tree peony I'd ever seen. On the ground around it lay light blue forget-me-nots and a mass of other springtime perennials, some blooming, some in bud.

Hosta blooming white, lavender, and violet and brilliant pink bleeding heart flowers filled stalls where horses once lived.

In another stall, gold koi lurked in a pond amidst rocks and papyrus.

In yet another, a green and gold garden plaque floated above a floor of emerald groundcover and declared: One is nearer God's heart in a garden than anywhere else on earth.

Yes, I thought. And yes again.

Memory and reality overlapped with each other.

Memories of reading The Secret Garden to my children and watching and re-watching the movie with them.

A memory of older daughter, Nikisha, saving her hard-earned money from part-time work to buy a beautiful hardcover copy of this precious book for her younger sister, Lauren.

And, as I looked around me, a memory that the term 'paradise' originated in an old Persian word for a walled garden.

My throat felt tight, my heart beat faster. I was surrounded not just by beauty, but by magic as well. I reached out for Hamlin's hand, perhaps to reassure myself that this was no dream.

After a long silence I said something silly like "Wow ..."

But it was time to leave paradise and come back to earth. Without warning, the woman put her hand on my arm, as if we were old gardening soulmates. "You're obviously a gardener, too ..." she said softly. "So you can see how overgrown it all is."

She glanced around, fluttered a sad hand. "For the first time, my husband and I have been giving serious thought to selling it all. We're getting old, and it's foolish to keep a big garden like this. We love it, but we just can't look after it anymore."

It was long before dawn the next morning when an idea jolted me awake. I got up and wrote a letter to the owners of the secret garden:

> *Since you are too stubborn to sell me the irises and I am too stubborn to accept them free of charge, I hereby offer to garden for you this spring and summer. If you agree, you will pay me in flowers. We can start with the purple irises!*

At breakfast, my husband read the letter, roared with laughter, and called me crazy. But when he stopped laughing, he agreed it would be a good deed to help an elderly couple hold on to their beloved house and garden.

"You're a crazy woman, though," he repeated. "All that gardening for a patch of iris."

That's how I became volunteer gardener for Marion and her husband, Henry, two complete strangers. Twice a week or so — from spring to fall — I cleaned up their magnificent garden. Sometimes when I arrived I'd knock at their door to say hello and chat about the garden. Most times, though, I just did my chores and left quietly.

It was hard work. But gardening in the most beautiful and mysterious garden I'd ever known didn't feel like work. The birds and my own heart seemed to sing in harmony as I dug and clipped and planted and watered.

I was intrigued by two fig trees that filled a small glass greenhouse. Henry told me he'd kept the first tree inside their house till it got too big. Instead of getting rid of the fig, he built the greenhouse to protect it. From that tree, he cultivated a second, and now their branches threatened to overwhelm the glass.

"One of these days I will have to do something about it," he said.

I knew what he meant: he'd have to get rid of the fig trees he loved. I sensed that he'd been thinking this for a few years.

I once teased him that he was a farmer at heart. He smiled and said he came by it honestly. His family left Germany at the start of the Second World War and came to Canada to farm, he told me. First New Brunswick. Then Ontario.

"His must be a very interesting story," I mused to Hamlin one day. "To be German in Canada during the war couldn't have been easy."

Still, I didn't press for details. I respected Henry and Marion for their mix of friendly politeness and great dignity and didn't want to intrude. In spite of the fact that I'd been gardening for them for many months, I'd deliberately tried not to build a friendship. In fact, I still mostly came and went from their garden without stopping to chat.

You see, I never wanted them to feel obliged to invite me into their house.

Houses are for friends.

One day, out of nowhere, Henry and Marion invited us to supper.

We knew that Marion had been a chef for the Globe and Mail newspaper's excellent executive dining room. So we looked forward to the meal as much as the company.

Henry, who was in his late seventies, greeted us rather formally at the door. He wore a long-sleeved white shirt, dress pants, and dress shoes, presumably in honour of the occasion.

The two couples who dined together that night could not have been more different.

Henry was a semi-retired medical doctor with a slight German accent. A tall patrician in both looks and bearing. Hamlin was a TV news anchor in his forties raised in Canada, a former hurdler on the Canadian national track team.

Marion was a British-Canadian, pale-skinned, blonde. A gifted musician who gave piano recitals. I was Jamaican-Canadian, with brown skin and dark hair. I joked that the musical instrument I played best was the radio.

What we had in common, however, was a love of gardening. Our conversation started there, thick with talk of moles and cutworms, roses and delphiniums.

But the thing that made me happiest was the thing they never mentioned: that they'd stopped thinking of giving up their home, stopped thinking they were too old to handle the garden.

As the evening went on, it turned out that all four of us were concerned about the environment and our children's future in a changing world. But on the lighter side, we all loved to read, argue about politics, and tour old houses.

We sipped Henry's excellent wine and chatted easily. The evening was punctuated by laughter, stories, and fine food. By the time it was over, the difference in our ages, backgrounds, and skin colours simply didn't matter.

On subsequent visits, we learned more about them. Henry's family had left Germany when he was in his teens, having decided that they could not live under the brutal rule of the Nazis. But once in Canada, their German accents betrayed them every time they opened their mouths. Some people hated them. Many distrusted them.

Anti-German sentiment was so strong that Marion and Henry were married for a year before she even introduced him to her parents.

The love they shared sustained them through the best of times and what was truly the worst of times — the sudden death of a beloved son.

That evening during supper, as the four of us shared our life stories, I realized that we had become friends. Real friends.

We finally moved into our new home, roughly forty minutes' drive from Marion and Henry.

It was Frank Lloyd Wright-ish, but only in the most modest way. This was more Usonian model than Fallingwater, the architect's most famous masterpiece, but, in signature Lloyd Wright fashion, the small house was set into a hillside.

It was a one-storey structure with a flat roof and generous overhangs. Its front entrance faced lawn and trees on one side, and its back door faced woodlands, with a small stream flowing through the trees.

The house had been recently, and incongruously, covered in blue siding. In a fit of creativity, our family named it "the Blue House".

It was tucked into the woods, surrounded by lawns and trees, with no flowers in sight. Not a single trillium. For that you had to walk along the stream down into the woodlands and into the meadow, where you would find wildflowers of various varieties.

Christmas ferns, ostrich ferns, cinnamon ferns, sensitive ferns. Trillium and trout lilies. And yellow marsh marigolds. They stood not in patches, but whole colonies, covering hillside, meadow and wetlands, carpeting the floor of the woodlands, floating on the banks of the big stream at the bottom of the hill.

It was always a shock to return uphill to where the house stood and feel the bareness of the grounds surrounding it. Hamlin and I were gardeners. What would we plant in all this space?

Then, a few weeks after we'd unpacked, Henry and Marion showed up without warning, their car filled with more boxes and pots of plants than I could count. We gawked at hostas in various shades and sizes, then at the peonies, the cotoneaster, the King Solomon's seal. It was a multitude.

But most precious of all was a large box of purple iris.

As the months drifted by and another winter turned to another spring, our friends' gifts took root and blossomed around our new house. And the scent of flowers filled the air.

Seeds from Henry and Marion's forget-me-nots turned into mists of blue edging our garden beds.

The purple iris, named after the Greek goddess who rode rainbows, flowered in the late spring. And Hamlin and I remembered the grace of our friends and gave thanks.

CHAPTER 7
Not So Silly Rabbits

*Look deep into nature and then you will understand everything
better.*

Albert Einstein

It was springtime. We'd been living at the Blue House for nearly two years, surrounded by acres of woods, two streams, and a huge forest next door.

We'd created garden bed after garden bed of perennial flowers, herbs and vegetables. Hamlin had installed wooden fences from some left-over pickets and Nikisha, Lauren and I painted them white. The fence's heritage style didn't match the style of the house, but we didn't care. 'Left-over' meant they'd come with us from an earlier project; the fence cost us nothing but our own family's labour and a can of paint.

Everything was fine until the rabbits attacked.

I could never tell if it was always the same rabbits. They all looked the same to me. About the size of small cats, with tawny fur, white tails, enormous ears. Judging from the damage done, there must have been a whole army of them.

Now, don't get me wrong. We'd become used to rabbits and deer eating the tender stems of our flowering shrubs at the back end of our garden.

"They, too, have to eat," we said, proud of how well we were coexisting with the wildlife around our house.

But this wasn't a little nibbling on a flowering shrub at the back end of the garden. This was an all-out attack on Hamlin's organic vegetable garden. The garden he'd dreamed of. The garden he'd dug and fertilized, planted, watered, and watched over until seeds finally thrust up through the rich, black soil, reaching for the sun.

Spinach and lettuce, tomatoes, peppers and peas, cucumber, carrots, snow peas and beans. All in his own garden. Some for reaping and eating in the spring, most for enjoying in the summer and fall.

And now, in mid-spring, the rabbits were eating his snow peas and lettuce. What would the little beasts attack next?

Meanwhile, I had problems, too. The miscreants had attacked my perennial flowerbeds, chomping on the crocuses and tulips before they even had a chance to bloom.

"Mothballs," suggested a gardener friend.

"Cayenne pepper," said another. "They can't stand it. Makes them sneeze. Just sprinkle it around the plants."

"Have you ever seen a rabbit sneeze?" scoffed a neighbour. "You need to use human hair. Just gently push some strands of it into the ground around your garden beds. Works for squirrels, so it must work for rabbits, right?"

Wrong. We tried everything everyone suggested. Nothing worked.

"It's a rabbit epidemic this spring," Klaus, our neighbourhood expert on garden pests, declared. "The little buggers are everywhere."

Klaus, fed up with the damage done to his lawn each spring, regularly set traps for the moles that tunnelled through the soil and created mounds of dug-up earth on his precious lawn.

It was no use telling Klaus he was making a mountain out of a molehill. Those molehills bothered him no end.

A big man with a strong German accent, Klaus had some unusual ideas about gardening, many from "the old country."

But no, we told Klaus, we would not borrow his mole traps to place in our own uneven lawn. Yes, we said, we understand that mole hair makes great lures for fly fishing, but we don't fish.

All the while, he kept eyeing our higgledy-piggledy lawn, a look of longing in his eyes. And one day he asked if he could place one of his traps there.

"Okay," Hamlin said reluctantly, wanting to be a good neighbour.

The next day Klaus proudly brought over his trap: a vicious, medieval-looking iron contraption with long, sharp spikes.

I shuddered. The trap stayed there for some days. But I could almost hear the moles scream. We took it out, empty of captive moles, and returned it.

Still, you could always depend on Klaus to have some clever tactic for dealing with garden pests. He was in his front yard tending his lawn, which was suspiciously flat and un-mole-hilled, when I mentioned our rabbit problem.

"The local fox must have died … or moved on to greener pastures," he said. "Foxes are natural predators of rabbits. Whenever you see too many rabbits, it means the foxes aren't around."

So our question was answered. A shortage of foxes.

But how on earth do you find foxes and persuade them to chase away your rabbits?

It's true that we hadn't seen the local red fox for a while. Then, one afternoon, I followed the scent of rotting flesh through the trees at the edge of our property and there he was, his fur still a vibrant golden red, sprawled on the ground, very obviously dead.

I did the responsible countrywoman thing. I said "Yuckhh …" then held my nose and ran, leaving Hamlin to take care of the rotting carcass.

"Klaus was right," Hamlin said sadly when he came back from digging the grave. "The rabbits have taken over because the fox is dead."

The next day we checked our two gardens. Vegetable and flower. The tops of seedlings were bitten off, the flower bulbs uprooted and eaten. I wanted to weep.

"I've got it, Hamlin!" I said after a while. "We need to rent a fox!"

My husband gave me a withering look, shook his head, and muttered something, mostly to himself, about crazy women. Then he inspected the damage more closely and announced to the world, "When I catch that rabbit, I'll wring his little neck" — except that he used more colourful language.

After supper that evening, Hamlin showed me a magazine article. "It says here that foxes are indeed a natural predator for rabbits. But you don't need a fox. You just need its urine."

I'm not the swiftest woman around when it comes to catching on to new ideas. Like almost all of Klaus's ideas. And this one of Hamlin's.

"How on earth would you get fox urine?"

"At the hunting store."

"You're kidding. They sell fox urine at the hunting store?"

"Yes, it says here in the magazine that they do. Hunters use it to mask their scent when they go hunting."

I imagined hundreds of hunters roaming through the woods stinking of fox urine.

Turned out there was something called a game accessories store in a nearby town. It was a big store in a small plaza.

The place was full of the weirdest stuff. Everything you needed to kill something. Complete camouflage outfits including hats, jackets, trousers, boots, and hip waders. Enough camouflage to outfit a battalion of Special Forces.

A whole counter bristled with nasty-looking sheath knives. There were fly fishing rods and reels everywhere. Everything except guns.

It was mind-boggling. How could I have lived my whole life without knowing about such places?

And the customers. All white and male, all much older than us, all looking very comfortable in this strange place devoted to killing things. But we felt so uncomfortable, we must have stood out like fish in a chicken coop.

It wasn't difficult to catch the shopkeeper's attention.

"Err ... can I help you folks?"

Hamlin started to speak, then stopped and looked at me for help.

"Well," I began, trying to phrase the words just the right way. "We're told you sell fox urine ...?"

My voice trailed off, because once a woman has asked a man, a complete stranger, if he has urine to sell, there's not much more she can do. I half expected the shopkeeper to laugh.

He didn't laugh. "Yes, ma'am, we do! Fox urine."

I stared at the shopkeeper as if he'd confessed that the whole store was a front for Al-Qaeda. A couple of men in tartan shirts and camouflage trousers lined up behind us at the counter. One carried a particularly vicious-looking knife in a camouflage holster.

"You do?" For some reason, I didn't know what to say next.

Hamlin poked me in the side, which I translated as *Just go along, say thank you, and don't make a big deal about this. I'm feeling silly enough as it is.*

"We certainly do," the shopkeeper said again, as if he sold fox urine to people every day. Which, of course, he probably did.

"Ummm ... how much does it cost?"

"Seven dollars a bottle."

"It comes in a bottle?" Sometimes, my mouth has a mind of its own. What else would fox urine come in?

The shopkeeper grinned. "You want some fox urine, ma'am?" he asked. His voice seemed very loud. The two men behind us at the counter in tartan shirts and camouflage trousers muttered something to each other. One laughed.

"Yes … er … yes, please."

The shopkeeper came back with a plastic bottle about six inches tall with a picture of a red fox on the label.

By this time, maybe a dozen men in various articles of hunting clothing were lined up behind us.

The shopkeeper handed me the bottle. And that's when I asked the question of questions.

"How … how do you get the fox to pee in the bottle?"

By chance, it was one of those moments when nobody else was speaking. I swear there wasn't another sound in the entire store.

So everybody heard my question.

And everybody turned to look at me.

Now, if you've ever been the only white person in a sea of black faces, the only man in a lingerie shop, the only short person in a room full of giants — if you've ever been any of those things — perhaps you'll understood how I felt in that moment.

Hamlin and I were the only dark-skinned, non-fishing, non-hunting, non-middle-aged people in that entire store. Worse, I was the only woman in a store full of men buying stuff so they could go off into the wild to do manly things.

The shopkeeper's eyes opened wide. "Excuse me, ma'am?"

I could feel my husband staring at me. I could hear him begging me to spare him — and me — further humiliation. Hamlin was now a TV news anchor for the Canadian Broadcasting Corporation. Wherever he went, people inevitably recognized him. But he was a reserved man, an introvert. So he tried to keep a low profile when out in public.

I knew that my question was slightly indelicate. But we were in a hunting store, after all, and hunting is not a delicate thing. I was not going to back down.

My voice was firm, perhaps even a little louder than before. "I asked, 'how do you get the fox to pee in the bottle?'"

Time stopped. The two men in the tartan shirts and camouflage trousers behind us at the counter leaned forward to hear better.

Eventually the shopkeeper spoke. "Now that is a question I can't answer."

I couldn't think of anything else to say. The shopkeeper and I stared at each other. Neither of us blinked.

Hamlin, suddenly the gallant husband, moved in to save me. "Do you know if this stuff really works?"

The shopkeeper, relieved to talk to a sane person, said, "What do you need it for, sir?"

"To keep rabbits away from our garden."

"Seems to. A lot of people buy it for that purpose," said the shopkeeper. He handed me my change but avoided my eyes. "But you will have to reapply it after a rainfall."

Everybody turned to watch as we walked out trying to look as if we bought fox pee every day.

I'll spare you the discussion that took place in our car on the way home. All I will say is that it began like this: "Cynthia, I can't believe what you asked that man. 'How do you get the fox to pee in the bottle?' What on earth were you thinking?"

Back home, we sprayed the urine around the garden beds. It worked — but only until the next rainfall in what turned out to be a rainy spring and summer. So I had to keep returning to the store for more pee.

Alone. Because my husband's contribution to keeping our gardens free of rabbits was to declare, "I refuse to set foot in that store ever again!"

To me, the whole embarrassing thing was worth it for the glorious crops of vegetables we harvested from Hamlin's garden that summer.

It was worth it for the flowers that bloomed and blossomed in my garden.

And it was certainly worth it for the look — fear mixed with amusement — on the shopkeeper's face every time I showed up in his store.

Gardening, however, is much more than growing pretty flowers and nutritious vegetables. Gardening forces us to consider how we live with nature.

If you garden, and especially if you garden in the countryside, you will sooner or later find yourself clashing with the wild creatures that share our planet.

Hamlin and I had already cut down on pesticides and herbicides because we knew they poison "good" pests as well as "bad" pests. Some even kill bees and other insects that are needed to pollinate plants. And who knows what awful things they did to the vegetables we grew and fed to our family?

But there was still much that we didn't know about living with nature — or even about how nature lives with itself.

Until Hamlin read from that magazine article, it never occurred to me that there was a connection between the red fox that lived somewhere in the forest surrounding us and our rabbit-plundered gardens.

Nor did I ever have to research fox urine. I did it that summer mainly to find an answer to the indelicate question I had asked in the store. As I searched, I discovered that the fox farms and game reserves which supply it are regulated by agencies in both Canada and the United States. Which should mean that they're properly looked after.

But something about the whole idea of keeping these beautiful wild animals in pens made us feel uncomfortable enough to stop buying their urine. Using chicken wire and pickets, Hamlin instead made a secure fence around his vegetable garden, while I simply stopped worrying about the half-eaten flowers.

As for the moles in Klaus's lawn and ours? Klaus told us that the more he read up about the creatures, the less he wanted to kill them.

"They have a useful purpose in nature," he announced. "One of the things moles do is eat those pesky grubs in my lawn!" He'd learned that a five-ounce mole will eat nearly fifty pounds of insects and grubs — the larva stage of the Japanese beetle — in a single year.

Klaus's conscience clearly drew the line at grubs. But his remorse over the little underground creatures that damaged his lawn — and whose hair had provided a source of income — seemed genuine. As far as we know, he never set another trap.

CHAPTER 8
To Everything a Season

To everything there is a season, a time for every purpose under
heaven.

Ecclesiastes 3:1

Robert Montgomery might have had our home in mind when he wrote, "Home, the spot of earth supremely blest, a dearer sweeter spot than all the rest."

That certainly has been true of our homes, and especially now, of the Blue House. It's been the perfect refuge from two high-flying careers in the media.

Hamlin now hosted an interview show on television. I was a network executive who traveled around the world, helping other television leaders to improve their programs, helping journalists to make their stories more relevant and engaging.

But no matter how far away I travelled, family and home were never far from my mind. And so, to ease the loneliness, to bridge the distance, I wrote in my journal. And each time, after I returned home, I wrote again. It was a thanksgiving of sorts.

When I'm away from home, I can hardly wait to return. To Hamlin and our daughters, and our mother when she visits. To our pet dog Kinu, who sees no reason why he shouldn't share in the warm embraces with slobbering kisses, head rubs, and wagging tail.

Spring, summer, autumn, winter: this place is home.

Here, in this small blue house with no dining room, not enough closet space, and too-small bedrooms and bathrooms — in fact, almost everything is too small except the kitchen, the gardens and the great outdoors — my family feels at home.

The house rings with laughter, spirited debates, and occasional arguments, usually followed by hugs.

Surrounded by woods, we hang no drapes on the windows. It enhances the feeling that we are living, not in a house, but in the middle of nature.

We eat our meals at the harvest table in the kitchen where huge windows overlook the woods on one side, the small stream and more woods on the other.

EARLY SPRING

I particularly love this place in the early spring. Everything seems cooler, cleaner, with nature giving us a chance to start afresh. I can hardly wait to get out into the gardens in the early morning, to listen to the birdsong, and to inhale deeply, drinking in the fresh air.

The gardens seem more enthusiastic about life. Trees and shrubs and flowers and vines are vigorous, healthy.

The earth is expectant, pregnant with new life gestating in the soil.

New seedlings burst through the surface — some of which I didn't plant. This is part of the mysterious nature of spring in this place: you're never quite sure what you'll find in the woodland, the wetlands, or the garden beds. Which plants will make it through a rough winter? Which seeds, dropped by the birds or the breeze, will decide to sprout in our garden soil?

But some things are sure, every spring.

The little stream that runs alongside the house will swell with spring rain and runoff from the neighbouring land. It will gurgle and splash, becoming a waterfall as it makes its way over a series of rocks. Then it will continue downhill to join the large trout stream at the back of our property.

Thousands of ferns will rise from the earth and gracefully unfurl themselves till all you can see of the land on one side of our property is a huge expanse of light green fronds sloping down to the wetlands.

In the sunniest parts of the wetlands, large clusters of marsh marigolds will bloom a brilliant yellow.

The elegant weeping willows on the banks of the trout stream nearby will lose their slender leaves in the winter, but their long golden branches will sprout pale green leaves every spring. Willow and water seem to share a mutual attraction. The drooping branches reach for the water, as if engaged in some ancient ritual of the natural world. This place, this wondrous place, with its small blue house and acres of gardens both wild and cultivated have become — simply — home.

Our daughters think we're garden-crazy. Hamlin and I wholeheartedly agree.

"But this hobby keeps us at home, so we're only a shout away," I add.

They reluctantly agree that I may have a point. But both are at ages where they have better things to do than hanging around with their parents. Nikisha is an adult; Lauren is a teenager.

"I guess it's good that you're here at home and not out somewhere boozing it up like some parents," Lauren admits, shrugging.

If I'm fishing for further affirmation, it's the best I'm going to get.

"And the vegetables from Dad's garden are okay too," Nikisha adds.

It may sound a bit like a back-handed compliment but we accept their comments gratefully. We're crazy about gardening but we're crazier about our daughters. Hamlin and I do spend a lot of time in the gardens and their approval matters.

White hydrangeas — now turning light green — nod lacy round heads over the low stone wall that follows the curve of a long, serpentine garden bed to my left. There are exactly six hundred and seventy-seven rocks of various shades, sizes, and shapes in that wall. I know this because I placed them there one by one.

Hamlin, our daughters, my mother, and our friend, Tim, all helped me to "acquire" the rocks from nearby construction sites and farmers' fields.

"Put me to work in the garden," Tim had said eagerly, soon after he arrived from his home in downtown Toronto one weekend.

"Okay, come help me steal some stones," I said.

And so we drove to a nearby construction site and stood by the roadside, pretending we were admiring our surroundings while cars whizzed by us. Then when there were no cars, we climbed over fences to grab the rocks. Tim got to lug the bigger ones.

"Who was your slave last year?" he complained, as he lifted a heavy granite rock and heaved it into the trunk of my car.

Tim is a tall, sophisticated Englishman, and I am a short black woman. Some of my ancestors were actually slaves.

"It's retribution time!" I said in a bossy tone. "Time for me to get my vengeance for what your people did to mine. Go grab another rock and quit complaining!"

"Yes, ma'am," he replied dutifully, hopping to it.

In truth, some of those enslavers had been my ancestors too. My family descended from both the enslaved and the enslavers. But I wasn't going to let that detail get in the way of an act of retribution.

Tim and I were sharing the kind of banter that's possible only between people who have known and loved each other for decades. We barely noticed a car slowing, the driver staring at the open car trunk half-full of rocks and beside it, a short black woman bent over in laughter as the tall white man obediently lugged another rock.

I finished building that wall after two whole years of rock collecting. Two years of heaving and placing, two years of quiet scrutiny of the colour and texture and shape of each rock and how they all fit together, or not.

One day, I looked at myself and realized how strong my arm and leg muscles had become. Sometimes, the light of scrutiny also shone on the journey of my life, and why I was so determined to build this wall.

I had started the wall during a period of mourning – grieving over the deaths of dear relatives and friends. Then I went through whole stretches of anger – at God, at death, at life itself. But, near the end of the two years, I ended up in a different place. I found peace.

My family observed my silent odyssey -- watching and helping at times, but most often leaving me alone to carry on. At the end of it, they opened a bottle of champagne to celebrate.

Cynthia's winding wall had come to the end of its journey.

LATE SUMMER

The first morning after my latest return from a stint of work out of town, I can hardly wait to open our front door. This is one of the daily routines I miss when I work abroad during the gardening season.

Luckily, I have a considerate boss who allows me to work at home a few days a week after a trip.

It's early September. According to the calendar, not quite autumn. But the sweet, sultry days of summer are almost over. I breathe in deeply. The air is fresh and surprisingly cool.

A sheen of early morning dew coats the lawn between the garden beds.

I pick up my running shoes from their usual spot just outside the door, turn them upside down, and shake them out. The last time I forgot to do this, my foot encountered a soft, cushy frog. I don't know about the frog, but that's an experience that neither my foot nor I wish to repeat.

As I straighten up, facing the lawn, I see a scattering of grey and blue feathers. Bright red blood stains the grass under the bird feeder.

"Mindy!" I curse silently. "Mindy, you little wretch, you've eaten another blue jay."

I used to enjoy watching our own miniature version of the animal kingdom after I refilled the bird feeder. Chipmunks, rabbits, and squirrels would gather alongside the larger birds — doves and blue jays. Sure, they'd occasionally squabble and strut and threaten each other, but nobody ever got hurt. Now when they gather, I worry.

Mindy, our neighbour's sweet, lovable little kitten, has become a leonine predator. Any unlucky bird busy eating the seeds fallen from the feeder had better watch out.

"It's just nature," I tell myself. "Mindy is a country cat, and she's only doing what country cats do. Foxes eat rabbits. Cats eat birds. It's just nature."

I know it. But seeing the evidence is still a bit startling.

This isn't our first time living in the country. We've summered on a hundred-acre farm before. But here, nature seems so much closer, so much more immediate. Just a few steps from our door.

Early mornings, a family of white-tailed deer sometimes stops at our front gate, as if to say hello. Evenings, we hear coyotes howl in the forest around our property. And rabbits still like our gardens entirely too much.

EARLY AUTUMN

Autumn arrives and our family has much to do to prepare for winter.

Logs to chop and stack outside, because in winter we use the fireplace daily.

The oil furnace will need to be checked, rain water barrels turned upside down, outside water taps disconnected to prevent them from freezing and bursting.

And, of course, garden beds need tidying up. Some perennial flower-heads and stalks will be left in place to feed the birds. The wisteria vine will be cut back. And tons of leaves will be cleared from the lawn. This is where the girls are most helpful.

"No wonder they call it fall!" I yell to my husband and daughters. We are all raking what seem to be millions of fallen leaves into piles. We stuff each pile into large paper bags, watching out for Kinu, our pet Akita.

He loves to jump into our handiwork, creating a mess.

Nikisha, Lauren, Hamlin and I all take turns yelling at him but he looks so genuinely happy, we have to laugh.

Autumn is a busy time for the wild animals, too. Each creature must prepare for the change of seasons just ahead.

Our resident chipmunks scurry about their business, pause to watch me, decide I'm no threat, go back to work. A black squirrel, nut held in delicate front paws, runs across the lawn, stops to inspect me. Bright, inquisitive eyes. It sniffs and scampers off to wherever it stores food for the winter.

The fragrant, late-flowering clematis vine blooms against the dark wood of our old split-rail fence. Its small, creamy blossoms climb up one side of the fence, run over the arbour in between, and continue on the other side of the fence.

"You're a blessing," I tell the clematis. "Maybe you should give lessons to that bloomless wisteria in the back garden."

It's been several years since we planted the wisteria, dreaming of fragrant purple blooms. Hamlin even built a rustic arbour for it, using logs and branches of fallen trees. But the wisteria shows no gratitude, stubbornly refusing to bloom.

Our daughters tend to sleep in on Saturday mornings. Hamlin and I are up, quietly making ourselves coffee. Kinu, the gentle Akita giant, is wide awake. His tail makes a fast, happy movement; it would be called tail-swishing if it weren't so tightly curled.

It's time for his food and a long walk in the forest.

The three of us leave the house, Hamlin holding firmly to Kinu's leash. Autumn is our favourite time to walk in the forest. The bugs are gone. The air is fresh. There are still enough red, yellow, and russet leaves on the trees to provide a reddish-gold sunlight, yet enough on the ground to form a soft carpet over the paths in the woods.

Hamlin and I playfully kick up the leaves. Kinu lunges forward, trying to catch them. Often he stops to stick his nose right into a pile of leaves. His face, when it re-emerges, seems to smile. Sometimes, he rolls his whole body in the leaves and we stop and wait until he has finished his display of joy.

We've never walked through the forest in the autumn without remarking on the outstanding natural beauty of it all and how lucky we are to live next door to this piece of paradise.

As we walk back home, we notice that the plumes of wild sumac are much redder than they were just days earlier.

And now, even the wild cucumber vine blooms. I love its frothy cream-coloured blossoms, its star-shaped green leaves, and the way it clambers up shrubs and trees along our lane, displaying all its glory.

But everyone knows that once the wild cucumber blooms, short days and long, cold nights are just around the corner.

MID-WINTER

When your backyard is a forest, winter has its advantages. For one thing, you never have to worry about the deer flies and mosquitoes and other bugs that sting. For another, rarely do you encounter other humans.

Best of all: winter in the forest can be stunningly, piercingly beautiful.

> *So pure, so still the starry heaven, so hushed the brooding air,*
> *I could hear the sweep of an angel's wings...*

> Edna Dean Proctor

The moment my feet touch the wide path leading through the woods, I feel I am walking down the centre aisle of a vast open-air cathedral. The tall, snow-coated trees on either side of the path glisten in the sunshine. Soft snow underfoot — and nothing else. Or so it seems.

There is something so still about it that when we speak to each other, it is always softly, in fear of breaking the great silence of it all.

Ears are keener, eyes more attentive.

A vivid red cardinal on the branch of a bare-limbed white birch tree.

The sound of a woodpecker digging into the trunk of an old maple.

The flash of a chickadee flying between branches.

The sudden vision of a young deer, frozen stock-still in the pathway up ahead.

CHAPTER 9
Goodbye

*"My mother always talked to plants. I never imagined that one day
I would do the same. Perhaps my daughters don't imagine it
either."*

From my journal

Living in the Blue House for nearly a decade, we learned the sound, smell, and rhythm of the woods in spring, summer, autumn, and winter. We became part of nature, part of the forest. Or so we thought.

But ours was the old story of the family who moves to what it believes is the last unspoiled place within driving distance of the city — not realizing that thousands of other people will soon be doing the very same thing.

Development had already changed the village. Fields that once sprouted corn and hay were now filled with very new, very large houses and their owners drove cars.

When we first moved here, our home was only an eleven-minute drive to the commuter train, which took forty minutes to reach downtown Toronto where Hamlin and I worked. Now, less than a decade later, as the number of commuters multiplied, the roads were full of cars and travel times had doubled.

On some days, we spent up to four hours in train and car, often arriving home so tired and cranky that our family time was reduced, supper and conversation were rushed, and there was little time for an evening walk through the garden.

Bravely, we told each other that we'd survive this change. Bravely, we embellished all the advantages of living "closer to civilization" and praised all the special features of the house we'd bought. Bravely, we declared that we'd had the good fortune to live in paradise, which is more than most families ever experience.

And if our hearts hurt as we said these things to each other, we did not dwell on it. It was not a time to wallow in regrets. It was a time to say goodbye, and we planned to do it with dignity.

We took our final walks over the weeks before we left, each of us making our own vigil to a special place.

Lauren walked over to the big cedar and started climbing. Its massive branches supported the tree house in which she and her friends had played when she was younger.

Nikisha and Kinu walked the path through the forest, slowing their pace, marking their steps.

Hamlin meandered through the gardens. He paused under the large pergola he had built from fallen logs, reaching out to caress the posts, as if talking to them. Slowly, he strolled to the little studio he had built at the back of our property where he had spent many happy hours writing, reading, playing his guitar, listening to music. He closed the door behind him and didn't emerge for hours.

So much had happened in this place, so many memories made.

I walked through the garden, pausing at the memory of Nikisha and Tim's engagement party. I could see the guests seated at cloth-covered tables set on the lawn between flowerbeds. My heart swelled with pride and happiness all over again as I saw my daughter and future son-in-law, faces beaming with happiness, stopping at each table to receive congratulatory greetings and hugs.

A bit farther along, I came to the spot where Lauren and her friends had celebrated her sixteenth birthday. It had been a great party until two guests threw a plastic garden chair into the fire.

I shook my head, smiling at the memory, forgiving them for the adolescent foolishness that ended Lauren's party prematurely. This event and many others had now become part of family lore.

This place had nurtured our family's growth and creativity. Open to the great outdoors as it was, this home seemed to make our minds and hearts more open to possibilities. We could dream here.

All four of us had taken big risks in our time at the Blue House: Lauren at school, Nikisha in her career, and Hamlin and I, who made the biggest change of all. We left our television jobs, started a consulting company and, with Nikisha's help, launched an ambitious initiative to make our Canadian media more creative, more inclusive. Both were successful.

Would we once again bloom where we were planted? That was the plan.

I continued my journey through the garden now, stopping to talk to the flowers, shrubs and vines — even the stubbornly flowerless wisteria. I gave it a bit of encouragement and a gentle reminder that some vines and people are late bloomers.

"And there's nothing wrong with that," I said, not feeling at all foolish.

For a moment I felt just like my mother, who always talked to plants and trees and animals.

We sold our cross-country skis before we sold the Blue House next door to the forest. A final farewell to the miles Hamlin, Nikisha, Lauren, and I had walked, snowshoed and skied through the trees over so many long winters.

Goodbye, we said lovingly, to the little blue house with its acres of woods, streams and wildlife, its small blue studio and large wooden tree house.

Goodbye, we whispered to the great forest with its thousands of trees, the elusive red fox, the evening howls of coyotes, the legions of stars in the night sky.

Goodbye, we said to the white-tailed deer, remembering the days when a family of deer would stray out of the woods to say hello.

Goodbye, we said to the neighbours we'd come to know and like, to their children whom we'd watched grow into teenagers and young adults.

Goodbye, goodbye, goodbye.

Part 2:
GROWING WITH NATURE

CHAPTER 10
Old Farmhouse, New Garden

Its eaves are touched with golden light
So sweetly, softly shining,
And morning glories full and bright
About the doors are twining.

Paul Laurence Dunbar

Our new home was an old farmhouse on the northern edge of the city of Toronto. In well over a century, this property had been owned by only four families. It had been a working farm then an orchard, a hobby farm then a riding school.

The couple we bought it from, the fourth to own the property, had also kept horses for their family's riding pleasure.

As the years went by, most of the land was sold to builders. Now, the horses and barns were long gone, but the name remained etched into wood on a thick sign at the front of the farmhouse: Ambercroft Farm.

A large plot of land still surrounded the building, giving it the distinct air of being removed from the new houses that had sprung up near it. Less than an acre, but more than enough for even an avid gardener.

"One of these days, we'll have to move to something more adult, a grown-up house," I'd speculated to Hamlin just a couple years earlier as we took our evening stroll through the back gardens of the Blue House.

And here we were now, about to move into what our children called "a proper house", what Hamlin called "a serious house". Solidly-built, it had a red brick exterior. Inside, thick plaster walls soared twelve feet to the ceilings. Doorways and windows were framed with high-quality handcrafted woodwork.

The staircase was impressive, long and curving with a gleaming honey-brown maple handrail and wide steps.

"Perfect for Christmas garlands," our daughters declared as they eyed the bannister.

Nikisha and Tim had recently married and were living in Toronto. Lauren was completing her first year of university in the city. Our Toronto-based company was growing. All of that made the farmhouse location perfect: close enough to the countryside, but an easy drive to loved ones and office in the city.

If the Blue House had been a home for daydreams and a universe of possibilities, Ambercroft was a 'settle down and get on with it' kind of place. We were in the second half of our lives. It was time to seriously save for our retirement while also looking forward to becoming grandparents one day.

Ambercroft didn't need a sturdy white picket fence on one side of the property and a tall wall of cedars on the other to make it feel cut off from its surroundings. But it had both.

And there were trees. Towering blue spruce and majestic maples. Big, fat, dark-green pines. And apple trees: the two most enormous apple trees we had ever seen, both taller than the house.

The property also came with mature shrubs. They had names that hinted at bygone times and the colours of their blooms: bridal wreath spirea, ruby red wiegela, purple lilac and burning bush.

But there were no gardens at all.

"Well, what do you know?" Hamlin said. "We've once again bought a house with land, shrubs and trees, but no garden."

"We will create one," I answered. "We know how."

And the act of designing and creating a garden would bring us joy.

Even before taking possession, we got the owners' permission to dig garden beds around the sprawling front verandah as soon as the soil thawed.

Late April arrived. The sun was still weak and many of the days still cold. That didn't stop us from splitting our favourite plants in the Blue House garden and filling plastic pots for the journey to Ambercroft.

Hamlin carefully separated a sucker from the now infamous wisteria vine —

the same one that, in spite of all our hope and care, in spite of the large pergola Hamlin had built for it, had never bloomed.

"I figure the sucker's got about as much chance at blooming as the parent plant. Which is roughly a snowball's hope in hell," he explained, sighing loudly.

But he did it anyway, because in Canada's spring, people have hope and do strange things. And that's just the normal people. Gardeners are even worse.

Our friend Sandra understood the fever that gripped us, the need to have plants in the new garden. "I can't imagine you two moving to a place without your own garden."

That was the point. The new garden had to be in place before we moved in. "We'll bring you plants," promised her husband, Les. "How about some hosta? And lots of other stuff, of course …"

And so it came to pass that our friends gave us a veritable jungle of plants before we even moved into our new home.

Hosta, Solomon's-seal, pink flowering anemones, and a fern-leaf peony from Les and Sandra. Day lilies and a large pink bleeding-heart from Jean and Bill. Red poppies and plants without names from Gundy and Peter.

We had to work quickly. The homeowners had given us only three hours to dig beds and plant, and we didn't want to outstay our welcome.

Hamlin and I had fun working side by side. Digging and planting, tamping and watering, laughing and arguing over what should go where and why.

And then we'd finished it all and the new beds were planted. Some tall plants ended up at the fronts of beds while some small plants ended up at the back, but in our imagination, they looked marvellous when the warmth of summer came, and they bloomed.

We packed the car trunk with the garden forks and shovels and watering cans, as well as the empty pots and plastic bags that had contained garden fertilizer and topsoil. We came back to our new garden and had one last look around. Then we raced each other back to the car, laughing, happy, mission accomplished.

It was early spring, and we had just planted a new garden at the old farmhouse, and we felt young and in love.

Then, one perfectly calm and lovely evening in late spring my car was rear-ended on a rural highway. The accident damaged my head, eyes and teeth. But worse — for an ardent gardener — it damaged my neck, shoulder, back, and side, right down to my foot.

At first, I tried to ignore the pain. A gardener like me doesn't give up easily. But I could barely stand on some days. Instead of spending happy hours in my new garden, I spent months in bed, then years on drugs and physiotherapy, then back in bed again. Anything to fight the pain. Anything to get better.

Back in the exciting months before we moved into the new house, back in the time of daydreams, we'd planned to build two garden arbours so my clematis vines could train over their frameworks and seek the sun.

Lying in bed in the early years after the accident, I finally gave up on that plan. For a while it seemed that Hamlin would abandon our garden dreams, too.

But Hamlin, the vegetable gardener, the same person who'd once sternly asked me, "Can you eat flowers?" was refusing to surrender.

From my bed upstairs in the house, I watched him build the first arbour — a simple structure with a curved top, positioned as an entrance to a garden bed on one side of the back lawn.

And then he built the second.

Day after day, as spring turned to welcome summer, whenever he had spare time, he was out there in the garden, cutting and hammering, staining wood, slowly building latticework for the tops and sides.

I watched him dig the post holes, lift the latticework and its supports, until the arbour stood tall in the middle of the back garden.

Then I watched him plant the clematis vines.

And as the weeks and months slipped by, I watched the clematis slowly climb the arbour's latticework, first just vine stems, then tendrils, then leaves and buds, then — finally — gorgeous, round, pink and purple blooms open to the sun.

And as I watched the clematis grow, I smiled. And when it bloomed, I laughed with joy.

The arbour, dressed with its flowers, looked like a place where a bride and groom would exchange vows.

Our older daughter had celebrated her engagement in the gardens of the Blue House. Perhaps, I thought, we would witness our younger daughter's wedding ceremony right here one day. Or perhaps Hamlin and I would renew our own wedding vows here. One day.

But there's more than one way to renew a pledge of love.

Sometimes, as he was building and staining and planting, I looked at my husband and wept. He was sending a message, and I got it.

My arbours — and the clematis vines that graced them — were labours of love. Hamlin's love for me.

More than that — it was a message that I shouldn't give up on our dreams.

That one day, I would be whole.

That one day I would stroll, pain-free, in my garden, my husband at my side. And that together we'd sit under the flower-covered arbour he'd built, sip a cool drink, and share our daydreams in the garden we tended together.

One day.

CHAPTER 11
The Woman in the Window

*He who would have nothing to do with thorns must never attempt
to gather flowers.*

Henry David Thoreau

E ven from my "hiding spot" behind the mullioned window of our bedroom, I
could see the couple. Arm in arm, the woman and man walked leisurely on
the sidewalk that curved on the other side of our long garden fence.

They seemed extremely well-dressed for an evening stroll.

They reminded me of couples I had seen on the beachside promenade in San
Sebastian, Spain. Middle-aged couples taking their evening walk, some with
their grandchildren, everyone dressed up from head to toe, as if attending an
important event.

I was there on television business one May and had dressed casually, which
seemed an appropriate choice for a walk.

On the nearby beach, some people lay nude, perhaps trying to get a late-day
tan in the still warm sunshine. But on the promenade above them walked
women, men and children, fully and elegantly clothed. I wasn't sure which sight
surprised me more.

In Italy, which I also visited on business, they called the evening stroll la
passeggiata.

A walk from my hotel to the centre of Florence could take forty minutes or
so, depending on how many times I paused along the way. I'd stop to look at the
waters of the Arno, the river that flows through the city, or to admire the grand
double doorways of some old Florentine homes and wonder who lived there.

Sometimes, I'd stroll through a piazza, scrutinize the statues and mischievously imagine the words they'd say to each other if they could.

Some days, worn out from long meetings about the state of the television industry, and badly missing my family and home, it wasn't dinner I looked forward to most, but the evening stroll. La passeggiata.

Time split into two on that mild spring evening of the car accident. Before I even knew it, a solid wall had sprung up, separating my life into before and after.

As if to make the difference less real, I shortened their names, especially in my thoughts. BA: the time before the accident. AA: the time after the accident. But I could feel it inside me. It was as if I, too, had split into two.

Happy and interesting events were on the far side of the wall. The active times with my husband and children. The taking on of difficult challenges that almost always led to successful outcomes. The travel to interesting cities.

They firmly belonged in the time before the accident.

Hanging out with my now-grown children; shopping for clothes with my mother and sisters; gardening, dancing and taking long walks with my beloved. BA, all of them.

The gardens I visited now were few, all belonging to close friends. Friends like Jean, Carol, Linda and Jessica, who (as I told my journal), "pretend they're not sticking close behind, watching over me, but who sometimes give themselves away when I stumble and my heel lands on their toe."

I watched the beautifully-dressed couple now as our garden came into their full view. I knew they would suddenly stop, as if awestruck; it's what many others had done. After all, it's what Hamlin and I would have done at the sight of a beautiful garden. Had done, many times. BA.

They did. I couldn't see their eyes, but I imagined that they were as wide as daisies. The woman looked around, as if making sure no-one could see her. Then she stepped closer to the sturdy picket fence, leaned over, turned back to her husband and clutched his arm as if to say, "Come and look at this!"

Standing side by side, they peered at the lush garden beds, shaking their well-coiffed heads, smiling at what they saw and then at each other.

Below them, the garden was fragrant, blooming in colours of pink, blue, yellow and cream. The yellow and cream came from the honeysuckle flowers, which always gave a fresh citrus scent.

The woman turned her head upward and to the left, as many others had done, to stare at the tall arbor. She seemed spellbound.

It was the best time to see the wooden structure Hamlin had built over the garden gate to accommodate the two clematis vines that thrived there. Blue flowers on one side, pink on the other, the vines reaching up toward the arbour's trellised roof.

Something in the way the woman moved her head alerted me: she was now looking straight at the window where I stood. I pulled back, knowing I could still see her but she wouldn't see me. I had done this so many times in recent years, I had perfected the art.

I was the woman in the window, the shadow whom passersby might glimpse once, but a second later, weren't sure they had seen.

I smiled as the couple admired our garden, pleased that the sight of our home was giving them such pleasure.

They stood there for so long that I went to lie down on my bed. When I looked through the window again, they were walking away slowly, still gazing at the garden as if reluctant to leave.

I wondered briefly who they were. And I wondered what stories they imagined beyond the fence and behind the walls of the beautiful old farmhouse on the corner.

Did they create a story about who lived here? Did they wonder what it had taken from the owners to create such a beautiful garden?

I was sure they couldn't guess the truth: the tangle of blessings and hardships that lay beyond that fence, in those garden beds and behind those walls.

How were they to know that a man and his wife had created most of this garden in a few hurried hours, their hearts full of hope and excitement for the future?

No, I thought. I would not have wanted them to know the truth. But a saying of my mother's drifted into my brain. For a moment, I found myself wanting to tell it to the couple, though softly and kindly and only just in case.

"Never envy others. You never know what they're dealing with."

CHAPTER 12
The Garden of Acceptance

Gardens are not made by singing 'Oh, how beautiful,' and sitting in the shade.

Rudyard Kipling

For years, I'd been a wife, parent, community volunteer, and high-ranking executive, mostly at the Canadian Broadcasting Corporation.

During these years, the garden helped me to unwind, find peace, get closer to my own heart and maybe even to God's.

Gardens have a way of giving generously.

My hands adored the texture, the rich, damp, life-giving smell of the soil.

Every spring I planted. And every summer I rejoiced as my flowers grew and blossomed.

Every autumn I planted again. And every spring I marvelled at the miracle of plants thrusting up through the soil towards the sun.

New life.

Over the years, my garden knowledge and confidence grew. I became more and more at home in my garden. I knew what I was doing, knew how to spot a sick plant and often how to nurse it back to life.

I'd never walked through any of my gardens without bending down to inspect something, deadhead something, yank a weed from the soil. Or to dig up a crowded plant needing sun and space and move it to a better spot where it could thrive.

Gardening made me stronger. It toughened my body, helped sort out my mind. During my precious time in the garden, big problems became small problems — or at least, more manageable.

My soul exulted in my gardens. That old saying sometimes came to mind, that one is closer to God's heart in a garden than anywhere else on earth.

Then came the accident.

Now I couldn't garden.

Now I couldn't find joy in the feel, the smell, the loamy richness of the living soil in my hands, between my fingers.

Now when I limped and stumbled through the garden, I couldn't work in it. Couldn't kneel as if in prayer, marvelling at the life of it, wiping the sweat off my brow with soiled hands, muttering to myself, sometimes replying to myself, hoping I wasn't going crazy, but not caring. Not one little bit.

I couldn't tend my own garden.

I was like a mother unable to tend her own child.

So many things that needed attention. So little I could do about them.

No moving the fragrant blue forget-me-nots that strayed into the lawn like truant children who went out to play and forgot to return home. Descendants of the same forget-me-nots I used to dig out with my trowel and replant at the front of a garden bed where they'd bloom as if they'd been there all along.

No dividing the mature hosta to create three or four glossy, big-leafed plants to dig in where there's more shade than sun.

No cutting back plants grown so big they're choking out the little ones in front.

My husband did his best, of course. He listened patiently when I explained why the Annabelle hydrangea needed to be moved before it crowded out everything around it. And why rose hips should be left on the stem: birds love to eat them, maybe because they're rich in vitamin C.

And why this or that plant really needed pruning or replanting or feeding.

But since the accident, despite Hamlin's hard work, to my eyes everything in our garden looked unruly, higgledy-piggledy, out of control.

I tried to ignore the imperfections. But my frustration grew as each month passed.

Come July, it was as if the bright summer sun displayed all my sins for the whole world to see.

Spring's hope became summer's dread.

Words from the Book of Common Prayer came to mind: "I have left undone those things which I ought to have done ..." Followed by this grim thought: If you want to find out the definition of hell, talk to a passionate gardener who can no longer garden.

After many sessions at the rehabilitation hospital, I finally revealed that not being able to garden was driving me bonkers.

I told the therapists about the time I spread a blanket on the ground right in front of a garden bed, trying to dig out weeds while lying on my belly. My left arm and shoulder were painful and weak, but my plan was to use my right arm, which was strong.

"The problem," I said, "is that I can't see what I'm doing. I cannot turn my neck to the right. So it doesn't work."

I told them about another time when I sat on the ground, legs outstretched parallel to the front of a garden bed, trying to reach over my left side with my right arm to dig out a weed. I somehow managed to topple over into the garden bed instead and ended up with my face smack-dab in the middle of a host of pink lamium.

The therapists at the rehabilitation hospital listened patiently. They told me I needed to accept that there are some things I just couldn't do.

Acceptance. They kept using that word.

One said kindly, "This may be a good time for you to try container gardening."

"I've tried it," I replied. "It's okay, but not quite the same as gardening."

"Maybe this is a chance for you to see your garden in a new way," suggested another.

I stared back at her, feeling miserable.

"You really should sign up for the mindfulness and meditation sessions," a fellow patient suggested. "It will help you learn to accept the things you can no longer do."

The things I can no longer do.

I had gone along to get along, sure I'd hate the meditation sessions. I grew to like them instead.

rst I had to learn to let my worried thoughts drift through my mind without trying to stop them or judge myself.

"Thoughts are not facts," chanted the session leader. "They're just thoughts."

After several sessions, I got to the point where I could experience each moment without judging either it or myself. Without being angry at my injured body or weakened self.

When that happened, the meditation sessions did for me some of what gardening once did. While I was in a session, it calmed my mind, lessened my worries.

The therapists explained that for meditation to really help, it should be a daily practice, another tool to call on when pain strikes and worries surface. So they assigned the homework to us, their patients.

At home, I did the breathing and meditation exercises every day. And I told myself that not gardening was one of the things I just had to learn to accept.

"Maybe," I thought, "I can walk through my garden without judging it or myself."

So one late summer day, I gripped my cane for support and walked around the garden telling myself serenely, "It doesn't matter that the flower-beds have become a jungle. Instead, I will mindfully appreciate and enjoy each plant I see."

I surveyed the damage and said sweetly, "It doesn't matter that big plants seem to have literally swallowed up smaller ones. It's just nature being nature … a survival of the biggest. I must accept. I will accept."

And then I saw a big, awful, prickly, grey-green weed standing — flourishing — right in the middle of my flower-bed. The healthiest, biggest bloody plant in the whole border.

I wanted to scream.

I wanted more than anything on earth to rip the weed out. To crush it under my heel, cut it into little pieces.

But even if I could, I knew that I shouldn't.

Instead, I took a deep breath. Inhale, exhale. I reached down deep inside myself, used my new skill, let thoughts float through my mind. I searched for acceptance.

But the weed seemed to be smirking. Taunting me.

My new-found serenity took off and left me.

I screamed.

CHAPTER 13
Man against Squirrel

Discretion is the better part of valour.

A proverb

Way up in the tree is where the biggest, prettiest, sweetest fruit always grows.

I'd known this since childhood. Near my family home was a large guava tree, growing at the edge of a deep pond. Always, the best guava hung right over the deepest part of the pond – right in the middle. My sisters and cousins and I would watch the fruit wistfully, wishing we had wings.

I was having that feeling again one autumn day as I stared at a bunch of apples in the bigger of our two apple trees. A heritage variety, Wolf River, this tree was well over a hundred years old and still going strong. It was taller than our two-storey farmhouse, and right at its pinnacle was where the biggest apples thrived.

These apples were so far out of reach, they might as well have been guava hanging over the middle of a deep pond. That's why we always let the top apples go, no matter how big and tempting they looked.

Except the trees only bore heavily every other year, which meant that this was their "off year" and there were fewer apples than usual. This was the year when we had to compete with the birds and squirrels over who got first dibs at the apples when they started to ripen.

If we were lucky, the wind would blow some off the trees. Either Hamlin or I would pick them up and take them into the kitchen, where I'd cut around the bruised parts. I sliced up the rest and dropped it into the hot cast iron pot along with brown sugar, cinnamon and butter – a delicious filling for breakfast crepes.

But the very best apples were the ones that hung in the longest at the top of the taller tree. Which meant that we were now eyeing the dozen or so apples left up there. Still a creamy-pink, they weren't quite ripe yet, but when they were, those huge, fragrant apples could make quite a few pies.

"I'll use the tall ladder to get them when they're a bit riper," said my husband.

"It won't be tall enough," I said.

"I'll use the tall ladder, AND a long stick," insisted my brave guy.

Days later, I went out to the garden and looked up at the apples at the very top of the tree. But something didn't look right, somehow. There seemed to be a big bundle of leaves just about two feet above the best bunch of apples.

"You should go take a look," I told my husband when I came back inside the house. "If I'm not mistaken, that's the biggest squirrel nest I've ever seen."

He went to check it out, came back and said: "It's way bigger than it was last year. It looks double the size."

It was news to me that there was even a nest there last year. But maybe I was just dazzled by the abundance of apples in the fall. Between them, these two old apple trees bore thousands of apples in their 'on year'.

"It figures," I answered. After all, squirrels are supposed to be clever creatures, planning for the winter, and knowing, every spring, exactly where to dig for the nuts they buried in the fall. And, if you're a squirrel and you want to get the best apples on a tree, doesn't it make perfect sense to build your home right next to the source of your food supply?

I was suddenly wishing I were a squirrel. But the feeling didn't last long. I had apple pie on the mind. Right now, the squirrels were my enemies.

"You wretches!" I yelled up to the squirrel nest. But nothing moved. The nest remained still.

Meanwhile, the apples got bigger and redder every day. I couldn't understand why neither squirrels nor birds had got to them yet. Or my husband, for that matter. After all, he's the one who baked the pies every year.

But there was no sign yet of a ladder or long stick, or a husband getting ready to pick apples.

Mind you, he hadn't seemed exactly anxious to get going with the pies that fall. He'd been busy with work, perhaps forgetting that we had a whole bunch of relatives and friends who looked forward to his apple pies each year.

Days passed, and the only movement in the garden was by squirrels, birds, and a few wild rabbits.

For a brief moment, I wondered if my guy and the squirrels had made a deal. If maybe he went behind my back and promised the squirrels that he wouldn't touch the apples. Which would mean they could afford to bide their time, eyeing the apples and waiting till they were at their sweetest before chomping into them.

Man-Versus-Squirrel, The Movie, had suddenly become Man-Colluding-with-Squirrel.

Strangely, I felt relieved at this weird thought, because it seemed to me that in a fight for the apples, the squirrels would win. The squirrels were just a hop, skip and jump away from the apples.

But what if the squirrels were sitting there watching the apples with the same anticipation that we felt? Biding their time till the apples were ripe and ready? What if they ganged up on my poor husband when he was tottering on a tall ladder, aiming a long stick at that quartet of apples right below their nest?

I even imagined them gleefully pelting him with rotting apples that they had half-eaten and left on their branches near the nest.

"I don't think you should do this," I told him. "What if you miss and stick the pole into the squirrel nest instead? Those little wretches can be quite aggressive."

"It's red squirrels that are aggressive," he reassured me. "We don't have red squirrels."

But I wasn't convinced.

"I think we should be generous and leave those apples to the squirrels," I said, with a kindness toward God's furry little squirrel creatures which, in that moment, was totally false. "Let's stop by the farm market this week and get some Spartan or Spy or something else that's great for baking."

Husband looked at me, eyes narrowed speculatively, but finally agreed. I breathed a sigh of relief.

The final score was Squirrels: 12. Humans: 0. And that was perfectly fine with me.

CHAPTER 14
When the Must Turns to Wine

In wine, there's truth.

Pliny the Elder

A round the bend from our farmhouse, just a few houses away, lived Vito and
his wife Loretta.

Vito was somewhere in his late sixties, I figured. He was a good-looking
man with a full head of dark hair just turning grey. He wore large dark-rimmed
glasses.

If I saw Vito in his garden when I started my morning walk, I'd usually stop
to say hello.

Early on in our relationship, he'd asked politely why I walked with a limp
and a cane. I started to answer, stuttered then burst into tears, turned, and
limped furiously back to our farmhouse.

He never asked again. I considered this to be a great kindness.

Sometimes Vito gardened. Sometimes he just stood, leaning on a spade,
looking off into the middle distance. Vito was very good at looking off into the
middle distance.

He was also very good at talking and I was more comfortable doing the listening.
He spoke excellent Italian-accented English even though it was his third language. And
he had a huge knowledge of European history, wine, books, and gardening.

Of course, it was his gardening knowledge that interested me most. Even so,
I was happy to listen to whatever was on his mind before thanking him and
limping away.

I told Vito once that he spoke like a professor. He stared at me, maybe shocked because I'd mistaken him for a professor, or, more likely, because I'd actually uttered a whole sentence.

"No. Not me," he finally answered. "I am far less. I am an ordinary labourer."

He said the words almost wistfully, as if he would have really liked to be a professor but never had the chance.

Vito loved proverbs. Ask him about history, gardening, or wine and sooner or later, a proverb would appear.

He told me once that he bought grapes from vineyards and made his own wine. From crushing the grapes to wine — the whole process took several weeks.

I was curious. "When does the grape juice turn into wine?"

Everyone else I knew would have said, "Oh, around mid-November or so." Not Vito.

"Di San Martino ogni mosto e vino."

Vito knew that I spoke some Italian. But he also knew that on some days my mind was so groggy, I could barely speak English. He translated the proverb: "On St. Martin's Day, the must turns to wine."

When Vito was just a teenager, his family left southern Italy to work on farms and vineyards in France. From there they came to Canada, where Vito married the lovely Loretta and they raised their children together.

One day, I sat in their kitchen sipping a glass of Vito's homemade wine while Loretta washed dishes and put things away. Out of the blue, Vito confessed that for years he'd dreamed of buying the farmhouse my family now lived in. Mostly, he'd wanted the land, so he could plant his own vines and grow many vegetables. The vines would be used to make wine for family and friends, but he had planned to sell the vegetables.

"Maybe a little market stand in front of the farm," he said, picturing it in his mind even as he said the words.

But by the time the property came up for sale, he and Loretta had to admit they were too old to move. And too old to start their very own vineyard and market garden.

"I had big plans for your place," he told me, shaking his head as if to clear it of regret. "I would have had a huge garden for my vines and vegetables. A huge garden."

One day, Vito came to visit us. He inspected what we'd done with our new garden. Wide lawns, flowerbeds in the centre and on both sides. Hamlin's beloved vegetable garden discreetly to one side.

"All this land — and you have no garden!" Vito muttered.

I was hurt. "But I do have a garden." I pointed to my flower-beds. "There's my garden! Isn't it lovely?"

Vito muttered something in Italian. Then French. Then English.

"You have all this land — and no garden."

Hamlin diplomatically walked Vito away from my flowers, over to his vegetable patch. It looked great. The beets, onions, beans, and tomatoes were all ready for harvest.

"See. We do have a garden," said Hamlin proudly.

Vito looked at Hamlin's garden, looked at Hamlin, looked at me.

He shook his head.

He waved his hands to encompass our lawns. "All this land — and no garden." It was obvious that he thought we were barbarians. We had so much land. How could civilized people not fill it with vines and vegetables?

I pleaded for understanding. "Vito, I can't garden anymore. My back is in bad shape. And Hamlin has been so busy since I had the accident."

But Vito's disappointment overwhelmed him. He left, still shaking his head, his shoulders stooped.

"Think he'll ever forgive us?" I asked Hamlin as we watched him walk around the bend to his home.

"Don't know," said my husband. "But I know this much — I'm gonna make my vegetable garden a lot bigger come the fall. Much bigger."

Fall arrived. The maple leaves turned gold and scarlet and drifted down onto lawns and sidewalks and out into the road. It was a glorious mess.

The whole neighbourhood seemed to be painting, planting, and — most popular of all — preserving. It was the season for turning grapes into wine, tomatoes into sauce, apples and mint into jelly.

Across the street a neighbour bought half a pig and prepared it for curing. For months, big chunks of pork would hang from a long wooden stick in his cold room until they were fully cured. Then they'd become pancetta, capicola, prosciutto.

A few doors down, family members of all ages gathered in their garage to split enormous sweet red peppers in two, remove the seeds and stems, coat the glistening red chunks with olive oil, and roast them on the barbecue. The whole process makes the peppers sweeter when they're eaten weeks or months later.

Farther down the street, Paddy and Jacqui, who'd been the first to welcome us to the neighbourhood, were preparing their garden for the fall. They'd drop in to the farmhouse occasionally, offering Jamaican codfish fritters and mangoes, raspberries from their garden.

One day I surprised them with a jar of apple jelly in return.

I'd made it myself with apples from the trees in our garden.

"Make jelly," my therapist Sarah had advised one day after I told her about our heritage apple trees. "It will help take your mind off the pain."

Now, for most people, making apple jelly is reasonably easy.

You core some apples, cut them into quarters, put the pieces into a large pot with water, and bring to a boil. You let it all simmer for a few minutes, mash it up, strain it through cheese cloth, pour the juice into another large pot, stir in some pectin to help the jelly process, add sugar, boil again, skim off the foam, put the juice into bottles, and then sit down and have a glass of tea or wine while you watch it all jellify.

And there you have it. Apple jelly. Easy.

For me it was incredibly hard. Even though I'd made apple jelly lots of times before my accident, I couldn't remember a thing. I couldn't concentrate. The written directions didn't make sense. I couldn't remember which step followed which or where I was in the steps.

Slowly, agonizingly slowly, I cored and boiled and simmered, mashed, strained, stirred in pectin, added sugar, boiled again, skimmed off foam, put the juice into bottles, poured a glass of wine, and watched my apples, my very own apples, turn into my very own apple jelly.

I did it all by myself.

I was so proud.

For a few short months every year, Vito would be a vintner.

In late summer he'd start by purchasing the finest grapes he could find. He'd take them home and wash them before crushing them in a round, wooden, half-barrel–looking "press." The press sat on a huge metal saucer with a spout to drain off the liquid, and under that sat a container that caught the juice. Mash and juice together would be put into large blue plastic containers to ferment.

The process was always the same. Just like Vito's father and grandfather had done back in Italy: the fermenting, the straining, the waiting.

One morning I stopped to check on Vito's progress.

I played innocent. "I don't remember when the must will turn to wine."

Vito smiled and played along. "Di San Martino ogni mosto e vino," he said. On the feast day of St. Martin the must turns to wine.

Soon it would be mid-November. Time to pour the wine into demijohn containers, then let the sediment settle to the bottom again, then strain again. Several months later, the wine would be poured into bottles with the month and year marked clearly on the label.

Vito would taste the wine but not drink it yet — he usually kept the red wine for up to a year before using it. He was proud that it was "one hundred per cent wine" — unlike some vintners, Vito added nothing to the grape juice.

We were surprised that October when Vito came through our gate, carrying a large bottle of his own merlot. The bottle still bore the label of a fine whiskey, but that didn't matter, since Vito had clearly written, in pen, the word Merlot and the year across the label. This merlot was from last year's batch and ready for drinking.

I went out to greet him, using the moment to whisper sternly: "Now, Vito. No negative criticism about the garden, okay? Hamlin's worked very hard at it. Only critica positiva is allowed."

"Okay," he replied, eyes twinkling. "Only critica positiva." Hamlin thanked Vito for the wine and asked a little apprehensively, "Would you like to see the garden?"

We gave him the grand tour. I held my breath. As I'd expected, Vito ignored the flower-beds, walked right past them as if they didn't exist. But he smiled and nodded approvingly as he inspected the boundaries of Hamlin's expanded vegetable bed.

He was true to his word. He gave Hamlin good news, the critica positiva.

But I could almost hear him thinking: It's only a bit better. But who knows? Maybe one day they'll become real gardeners. Maybe even plant grape vines …

Hamlin smiled happily, and we went inside the farmhouse and unscrewed the cap of Vito's bottle of merlot and drank much of it.

We all agreed it was an excellent year.

CHAPTER 15
Bringing in the Sheaves

Season of mist and mellow fruitfulness,
Close bosom-friend of the maturing sun...

John Keats

It was October of the following year, and the harvest was finally in. Tomatoes. Eggplants. Peppers. Late raspberries. A lone pumpkin. Sweet peppers, not quite ripe. Garlic. Onions. Cucumbers. Zucchini, still yielding.

Out in the garden, the herbs still thrived. Chives, tarragon, oregano, basil, thyme and rosemary. Summer savory.

And mint. Always plenty of mint. Apple mint, black mint, mint balm, spearmint.

So much to give thanks for. From having a family and a home to having food to eat.

At this time of year, I was often reminded of something my mother used to say: "You don't have to be rich to plant a garden." No matter how little money our families had, my mother and my husband's mother always planted a garden. (My mother-in-law still did.) And I had lovely memories of the abundant produce that sometimes came from just a small plot.

The two old apple trees were laden with ripe fruit. Their red, pink, and yellow gleamed bright through the green leaves surrounding them. They're heritage apples. Wolf River. Big as grapefruit, yet fragrant. Sweet, yet tart. An old variety, but a fresh, new taste.

Dozens fell every day. Some bruised, even though the grass below was thick and soft. These were used to make jelly and pies. Hundreds of others — firm, ripe, perfect apples — we gave to neighbours and friends.

In a fit of late-day ambition, the pumpkin vine even flowered again and put out several perfect tiny pumpkins. It was a Jamaican pumpkin, grown from a seedling that came from neighbours Paddy and Jacqui.

Pumpkins in Jamaica were big, with several on one vine. Come to think of it, pumpkin vines everywhere — including right here in southern Ontario — seemed to yield several pumpkins.

Not our vine. Only one of its pumpkins made it to maturity this summer. As if to make up for that lack, the vine was trying again — in early October. I thanked it for the effort, but warned that it was engaging in a lost cause.

"You're in Canada now," I told it — one of the foolish one-sided conversations I tended to have with plants and shrubs when I walked through the garden. "Cold weather is just around the corner."

But last time I checked, the vine had sent out yet another flower atop yet another tiny pumpkin.

Ridiculously exuberant over the one mature pumpkin it gave us, we decided to treat it as a whole crop. So we called Paddy and Jacqui to come get their share of "the pumpkin harvest."

"What about the bird pepper I gave you?" asked Jacqui soon after she came through the kitchen door.

"It got overshadowed by the asparagus and raspberry bushes," my husband said. "We realized it too late. It's just blooming now."

"But the raspberry bushes you gave us a few years ago are on their second or third yield this summer," I chimed in, wanting to atone for our inept treatment of the bird pepper plant and our failure to get more than one mature pumpkin.

Along with a half of the pumpkin, we gave Jacqui and Paddy tomatoes, herbs, and garlic. They smiled, laughed, and thanked us, happy with their share of the harvest.

The garlic bulbs were yanked out of the soil in late summer and left to dry in baskets and boxes. The biggest ones were given to family and friends like Paddy and Jacqui, the smaller ones left behind for our own use.

These garlic bulbs had grown by themselves each year. Untended, even unplanted, offspring of the seeds of a single garlic plant my mother-in-law gave us years ago. Who was to know that garlic was so easy to grow?

Before the garlic harvest, there was the red currant. For years the birds got to the currant bushes first, picking them clean before we got to them. So now we got to them first, leaving behind about a third of the crop for the birds. The result of that harvest was beautiful red jelly, a surprising combination of sweet and tart. Perfect with cheese, crackers, toast, ham or even to baste roast pork or chicken. Or Thanksgiving turkey.

Around the boundaries of our grounds, maple leaves were deep yellow. More turned red every day.

The leaves fell, drifted, settled. Perfect for dogs to bury their noses in. Perfect for small children — or adults with a sense of fun — to kick around, to crunch-crunch under their feet, to watch as a playful breeze scooped a few leaves high up into the air and carried them away to what felt like far-off lands.

I knew this time spoke of cold days to come. Of snow and ice and bitter winds. But I gloried in this cool, fall day, this splendid time of thanksgiving.

A blaze of warmth and glory before the brutal winter.

Inside, the old farmhouse glowed with warmth. Wood floors shone with the patina of age from a hundred and fifty years of families. And a hundred and fifty autumns just like today.

The furniture glowed — tables, chairs, the old hutch, the bookshelves all shone in the late-day light. Rays from the dying sun brightened the massive harvest table in the kitchen. My husband brought it home soon after we bought our first house.

Made of four thick maple slabs, eight feet long, the harvest table once served in the kitchen of a Masonic hall. Today it was covered with our own apple pies and jars of apple jelly.

A great basket overflowing with fresh produce from our garden sat at one end of the table. The kind of basket you still saw deep in the Jamaican countryside, hanging over the sides of donkeys, carrying mangoes, ackee, pawpaw, bananas, and avocados to market.

My mother gave me the basket, decades ago.

I stood at the stove, peered anxiously into a huge pot, watched the apple jelly bubble, bubble inside, and wondered: "Will it gel?" It didn't matter how many times I'd done this, I always wondered if it would gel. When it did, it was like a miracle, and I greeted the miracle with shouts of triumph.

On the other side of our kitchen, my husband stood at the harvest table, rolling dough. Today, he was trying a gluten-free dough for the first time and was as anxious about its success as I was about my jelly.

Will the pie crust be light enough, flaky enough? Or too much of both?

The smell of apples and cinnamon, apples and mint — apples, apples, glorious apples — filled the room. It reminded me of autumns past, when our children were small and I'd slice apples and chant "One for you … two for me" and give one slice to Nikisha and one slice to Lauren and drop four slices into the bowl.

Hamlin would mix my sliced apples in a bowl with mashed pears, cinnamon, nutmeg, sugar, and lemon juice. He'd scoop it all out and make apple pies, and the girls would bicker over who got to lick the bowl.

I looked forward now to their arrival. Both girls were grown up now, of course. With their own homes, their own loves, their own lives. But the scent of apples and cinnamon in the fall always brought back the memories.

Memories of the girls as children. Of family. And friends. And times loved.

"I am happy!" I told Hamlin. "Let it be remembered, when I am old and grey, that on this day, I was gloriously, completely happy!"

He looked up, still mixing the apples and the mashed pears, cinnamon, nutmeg, sugar, and lemon juice. He smiled. The sort of smile that said he understood and shared the feeling. But he said only "Yes …" and went back to the mixing.

"Yes …" I repeated. "I'm content … and thankful."

All around was the glory of the harvest, of the autumn, of remembrance.

And the joy of thanksgiving.

In our kitchen, in our home, and in our hearts.

CHAPTER 16
Listen to the Robins

Behold, my friends, the spring is come; the earth has gladly received the
embraces of the sun, and we shall soon see the results of their love!
Tatanka Yotanka, also known as Sitting Bull, Sioux Chief

It's five o'clock in the morning and the first robin sings on the nest she's been building in the shrub just below our bedroom window.

Cheerily, cheeriup, cheerio, cheeriup.Cheerily, cheeriup, cheerio, cheeriup.

It's such a welcome sound that I throw back the covers on my side of the bed and get up smiling, happy to greet the day.

"Spring is here at last!" I tell my husband. "Listen to the robin sing! Isn't it the loveliest sound?"

Hamlin growls something like "Uuuuurgh …" (it might have been stronger) and pulls a pillow over his head.

I grab my robe, head to the kitchen, make myself a mug of marvelously fragrant coffee (I seem to be smelling it for the very first time) and head out the side door into our garden.

My step is brisk, my spirit light. "Spring is here at last," I repeat loudly, as if telling it to the whole world.

The garden smells that wonderfully fresh, loamy smell that only comes after a good night's gentle spring rain. I smile. I laugh. I would skip like a teenager if I didn't hurt so much. I feel wonderful.

In patches all over the garden, the green spears of the first daffodils poke through the soil.

They're in the flowerbeds bordering the verandah. At the front and sides of the house. Under the evergreen trees just inside the white picket fence. At the front of flowerbeds. In the middle of flowerbeds. At the back of flowerbeds.

One daffodil shoots through the middle of Hamlin's vegetable garden. Obviously the contribution of an autumn squirrel that buried and forgot it. Or perhaps that remembered, after dragging it all that way, that squirrels really, really don't like the taste of daffodil bulbs.

Within a month the daffodils will bloom — yellow, yellow daffodil-yellow everywhere. Patches of wayward sunlight come down to visit the earth, to congratulate us Canadians for surviving our long, hard winter.

But the daffodils aren't the first ones to bloom in spring. That honour usually belongs to the smaller flowers — bloodroot or crocuses, some years both at the same time.

I've never understood why a flower as pretty as the bloodroot has such a grim name (even though its roots are undoubtedly red). It has such pretty, small white flowers, so early and so welcome in spring, and such charmingly unusual scalloped leaves. Couldn't someone have found a nicer name?

Never mind. Bloodroot cheers my winter-weary spirits to no end when I first spy its blooms.

But it's the crocuses that steal the show. And my heart. The Fairy Flowers of my childhood. A small flock of pastel-coloured flowers push their blooms up near the peonies, two or three more blooming each day. The crocuses flower in spite of the vinca minor groundcover that keeps trying to steal their territory, no matter how many times I've yanked its creeping vine away. Easter Lilies is what my sisters and I called them back in Jamaica — so very long ago — when they bloomed in a very different spring in Mama's garden.

"Hello there, Easter Lilies," I say to the crocuses each morning. "Nice to see you again."

If there's one time of year when a mostly sane person is totally justified in talking to flowers, it's early spring, right after a long winter.

On the newest arbour — the one that Hamlin built for me over the side gate — the clematis is always the first vine to bloom. Against the white lattice, its fuchsia-pink flowers nod a happy greeting to all who pass by.

"Good morning, clematis," I answer. "And how are you this fine morning?"

It will bloom again in late summer, just after its companion clematis has given us a lengthy show of blue-pink flowers.

To the left of that arbour, sprawled across the sturdy white picket fence, is the wisteria vine that bloomed twice and decided to quit. We've tried everything. More water. Less water. More fertilizer. Less fertilizer. Once, on the advice of a very experienced gardener, we even cut into a root to shock the vine.

When all that failed, as long as there was no one around to hear, I descended to begging, bribes, insults, and, finally, ominous threats of uprooting and throwing it on the compost heap.

Nothing I said, of course, made any difference.

It's now a mature twenty-three year-old. And still each year I hope for blooms and fool myself into thinking the unfurled leaves in early spring are really blossoms just waiting to bloom.

I've even taken to writing silly poems about this wisteria, running all the way from secret hope to sad disillusionment.

My first poem became popular with fellow gardeners, perhaps because it has lines like "Wisteria, oh Wisteria / You drive me to hysteria".

Not exactly William Wordsworth, I know. And if you think that's bad, be assured that last year's poem was worse: "Wisteria, you odious vine / You are no friend of mine ..."

I imagine my tombstone with these mournful words carved into it: "She succumbed to grief over her bloomless wisteria and hapless poetry ..."

But let us not dwell on failures. A new spring is a time of hope. Hope that the long winter is past, and that the summer will be heaven. Hope that the gardening season will be joyous, with just enough sunshine and just enough rain, and not too many aphids, cabbageworms, earwigs, or mosquitoes.

Our quiet neighbourhood comes to life each spring. Lawns are fertilized. Chairs — and people to sit on them — suddenly appear on verandahs again. People rake lawns. Pots of pansies are placed on the sides of front steps. Their cheery little faces, in yellow, blue, and sometimes both yellow and blue together, seem to smile at everyone who passes by.

Neighbours greet each other, some for the first time since early winter, back when we all migrated indoors and closed doors and windows against the cold.

Conversations now are almost entirely about the weather and gardens.

"Thank God the winter is over! Can you believe how harsh it was?"

"Yes, and there's still time for a killer frost ..."

"How's your lawn doing?"

"Some patches where the moles did their damage. But they eat grubs, so let's not complain too much."

"But the rabbits! So many rabbits! I'll have to put a fence around my back garden this spring!"

"Have you tried hot peppers? Or fox pee? I know a place …"

On and on it goes. Unless it rains too little or too much, which gives us something else to complain about. With gardeners, conversations always seem to come back to the weather. And everyone in our neighbourhood, it seems, is a gardener.

I remember the criticism about a family newly arrived in the neighbour-hood.

"They're not tending their front garden," complained their neighbour directly across the road.

His tone sounded just like he was saying, "I suspect they're axe murderers." Around here, it's a terrible crime to not tend your front garden.

The neighbour directly across the road should have held off on his criticism.

One gorgeous day, as Hamlin and I walked past with our dog, there was the new neighbour planting seedlings in a bed he'd dug in front of his verandah.

I could have told him the day was too hot to plant flowers. And that he shouldn't line up his new plants like soldiers all in a row. But instead I smiled a warm hello and asked him what he was planting.

"I'm not too sure, but the garden centre said it would flower throughout the summer."

In his voice were the pride, hope, and uncertainty of new gardeners. That summer he was in his yard nearly every evening, mowing his lawn and tending his new flower-bed (turns out he planted geraniums, impatiens, and gladioli).

Hamlin and I encouraged him every time we passed, delighted that he'd proven our neighbour so wrong.

In May of every year, Hamlin starts his vegetable garden. Spinach, lettuce, and garlic first, followed by onion, tomatoes, zucchini, potatoes, and beets. Then a bunch of other vegetables and herbs. Planting time is his busiest time in the garden.

I tease him that he's a stereotypical guy. "You plant the seeds, stick around just long enough to make sure they're established, then leave me to do all the nurturing and watering."

Hamlin suggests it can't be that hard to pick an occasional weed or turn on a hose, then turns back to the book he's reading.

My ideal spring is when it rains just enough to keep the sprinkler turned off, but not so much that everything in the garden looks drowned. My ideal spring is when the sun shines enough to grow the plants, but not enough to scorch them.

But the truth is that my ideal spring is spring itself.

I'll put up with the voles and moles in the lawn, the rabbits, the mosquitoes, and even too much rain, as long as spring arrives, bearing its gifts — the sights, smells, and sounds that herald a whole new beginning.

Remember how I started this chapter welcoming the song of the first robin in spring?

My delight doesn't last. Within a few weeks, when the robins start their dawn song, I cover my ears with a pillow, just like Hamlin, and beg them to stop. "Enough already! Please let me sleep a bit longer!"

They don't, of course. Not for several long weeks.

Then one day around the end of May, robin fledglings flutter out of the nest under our bedroom window tilting unsteadily for the garden, and we can sleep a little longer.

But that's not the end of our relationship with the robins.

Turns out that for the first couple of weeks after the fledglings leave the nest, they aren't noticeably good at flying. And robin parents are very protective of their offspring. So, while the baby birds flutter around rather helplessly, the parents dive-bomb anything that might threaten them.

Including cats and dogs.

And Hamlin and me.

I have no doubt the robins would dive-bomb a bear if it got too close.

It's no use reminding them that my family owns this property, and they're only tenants. Apparently, protecting their progeny around the large shrub next to the pathway has given them full rights to decide who should enter that area.

Hamlin and I enter at our own risk.

But it's spring.

And flowers bloom.

And robins sing:

Cheerily, cheeriup, cheerio, cheeriup.

Cheerily, cheeriup, cheerio, cheeriup.

And the world is suddenly a better place.

CHAPTER 17
A Bloomin' Competition

Spring has returned. The earth is like a
child that knows poems by heart.
Rainer Maria Rilke

S pring. The end of winter. A time of blooming bulbs and happy thoughts. And the annual competition with Les.

Les has been my good friend for many years. Several of the plants in my garden are gifts from him and his wife, Sandra. But in early spring, we're garden rivals, locked in a fierce battle.

Who will win The Bloomin' Bulbs Competition this year?

Who'll be the first to enjoy butter-yellow daffodils, their trumpets waving in the spring breeze? Blue scilla, tiny flower-heads nodding at the ground below? And hyacinths, in white, blue, and pink, their fragrance sweet on the air? And tulips, of course, in so many cheerful colours?

Who will be the first?

It's our equivalent of the Stanley Cup. The Super Bowl. The Olympics. All rolled into one.

Les lives in downtown Toronto, where Lady Spring tends to put in her first appearance, while I live in the frosty northern city limits. If he wins the competition, I will complain that the difference in temperature gave him the edge.

If pushed, I will admit that there are a few mitigating factors. Though the temperature is warmer in Les' part of town, his garden is several feet from the house and gets no warmth or protection from it. Also, it's partly shadowed by trees, so it never gets a full day of sun.

My bulbs, on the other hand, get full sun and many are planted close to the house, giving them both warmth and protection.

All of that makes it a fair fight. But I only mention that fact when I win. When I lose, I cry foul.

This competition is serious business.

A spring garden competition is no place for sissies.

And so every spring morning I wake with the birds, anxious to get out into the garden. Down the stairs and out the side door, eager to see if anything is blooming.

The first several days are always a disappointment. The flowerheads get fatter and rounder, but there isn't even a hint of colour.

I head over to the back garden, check a patch of crocus. Crocus is normally the first to bloom.

Nothing yet.

A day later, Les phones to announce that he has snowdrops blooming.

I'm devastated. "Snowdrops!" I splutter. "You never admitted to having snowdrops. In fact, how do I know if that's true? I need photographic proof!"

"Not to worry," Les replies. "Snowdrops are winter flowers, so technically, they don't count."

"Hmmph …" I reply, mollified. "Okay, then. Snowdrops are winter flowers. Good to know."

"Have a good day," Les says cheerfully and hangs up.

I regard this exchange as a splendid example of decency, integrity, and honour. Roughly the same as one of my daughters admitting she ate the chocolate Easter bunny before the appointed day.

The next day, I notice that the daffodil heads are showing a bit of yellow. This sets my heart aflutter. But closer inspection reveals that this isn't the full-blown yellow of a daffodil in bloom, but a kind of chartreuse — a greeny-yellow — meaning that the flower isn't quite ready to bloom.

For a moment, I wonder what would happen if I use a hair dryer to warm the plants' roots. I'm tempted. Lord, how I'm tempted! But that would be cheating. And I won't lower my standards.

Instead I urge the daffodils, "Hurry up! Hurry up!" And will them to bloom.

Back inside the house, I start dialing Les's number. Then I catch sight of the clock and hang up quickly. It's only six-thirty. Even I am not crazy enough to phone someone this early in the morning.

At eight-thirty I phone. Les's wife Sandra answers.

I'm scared. "Good morning, Sandra. It's your Bloomin' Competitor calling! Is there anything blooming in your garden today?"

"I'm pretty sure not," Sandra says. "But I'll get Les to the phone."

Les sounds calm, unruffled, in sharp contrast to my feverish tone. I'm pretty sure it's all an act.

"Now, please don't tell me that all your daffodils are blooming," he says in his droll way.

"Not quite, young man." (Les is a couple of decades older than me. I usually call him "young man" when I'm trying to be authoritative.) "But don't count your chickens yet. Anything could still happen. It's supposed to be a sunny day today!"

Les laughs. I laugh. Neither of us really believes we'll get blooms today, but it's important to keep the pressure on. We wish each other a good day and hang up.

Nothing blooms that day. Lady Spring has suddenly gone very cool and everything in the garden slows down.

The next day my daffodil buds are a brighter yellow. But they're still not open. Scilla seems on the verge of blooming. But not quite yet. Crocuses have bright green leaves with white stripes down the middle. But no blooms. Hyacinth flowerheads stay closed tight.

This isn't looking good.

While I wait for a decent hour to make my daily call to Les, an e-mail drops into my inbox.

There's a message and an attachment.

I have a premonition, open the attachment first.

Photographic evidence that daffodils, scilla, and tulips in yellows, pinks, reds, and blues are blooming in Les's garden.

I want to cry.

I read the message.

"So sorry about this, chaps, but we are awash in spring blooms."

There's no question. Les has won The Bloomin' Bulbs Competition.

I'm humiliated. I must now graciously concede defeat. It's the decent, honourable thing to do.

But just as I'm about to send a surrender message, something in the picture catches my eye.

"Are those …? No, they couldn't be."

I look closer, enlarge part of the picture.

"Have a look at the photo Les sent us!" I holler to my husband, who's working on a script just a few feet from me.

Hamlin looks at the computer screen. "It's really beautiful." He tries to cheer me up. "Guess this is what happens when you have a garden downtown."

"No. No. Take a closer look. What's wrong with this picture?"

He leans in, stares at the photo, pauses. He shakes his head, roars with laughter.

"I don't believe it." There's a look of admiration in his eyes. Not for my detective skills, but for Les's clever, mischievous deceit.

Les answers the phone on the first ring. It's as if he's been sitting there, just waiting for my call.

"Good morning, Cynthia," he says innocently. "I guess you got my photograph. Ready to concede defeat?"

"I nearly did," I reply. "You had me fooled for a few seconds."

"I don't understand," he says even more innocently. But it sounds as if he's trying not to laugh.

"You wretch!" I can't help laughing. "You nearly got me with those gorgeous blooms!"

"What gave it away?"

"I know your clematis …" I'm triumphant now. "I know that clematis of yours, and it doesn't bloom till much later!"

"Well …" he says in that teasing voice I know so well. "It was worth the try. And it nearly worked." He pauses, asks carefully, "So … is anything blooming in your garden this morning …?"

I consider cheating. Decide I've got the moral high ground here and want to keep it that way. After all, I'm a gardener, and gardeners have a certain code of honour. "No. Nothing blooming. But very, very close." I pause. "But tell me, Les … would you have confessed?"

He laughs. "Of course."

I will never know.

As it turns out, we both get our first blooms the next day. Three crocuses in my garden. A few early tulips in his.

This year's Bloomin' Bulbs Competition is a draw.

We decide our rivalry is foolish and childish and unworthy of such mature adults as we. And immediately place a bet on which of us will have the most blooms by the end of the month.

And I do have to admit that Les has proven to be my muse for some of the silliest garden poems I've written. He's not the only one.

Cynthia Reyes

Ode to a Boastful Wisteria Owner

My good friend John
The gardener one,
He boasts of his wisteria.
He calls me once,
Then twice, then thrice,
He's this close to hysteria.

"Tis blooming now!
Come see, come see,
The buds are getting fatter!"
John keeps this up
All summer long,
A never-ending natter.

The problem is
John's vine does bloom
And mine again is fallow.
(It's come to this
I find new words
For grief that I must swallow.)

John's vine doth bloom,
John's vine doth bloom,
Three times in every season.
"Come see, come see,"
John says to me,
Happy beyond all reason.

So off I go
Convinced he's wrong,
For now it is hot weather.
But Lo! John's right,
The vine doth bloom,
I'm fuming altogether.

It makes no sense
That it should bloom
While mine produces nothing.
But healthy hue
In leaves of green
It turns my mind to frothing.

Twigs in My Hair

Just now I get
Another note
From you-know-who, a-boasting,
And that is why
I write this verse
That John, he needs a roasting.

A clever plan
Has seized my brain
And now I start devising
A stealthy plot
To carry out
A bit of gardenizing.

Of digging up
My barren vine
And off we'll go together
In dead of night
Across the town
No matter what the weather.

And plant it where
John's vine once stood
And leave it in its glory,
While John's vine
Sprawls across my hood,
About to change the story.

Now we shall see
Who boasts each spring
And every single summer,
For John is now
Proud owner of
The world's non-blooming bummer.

CHAPTER 18
The Rabbits Attack — Again

Into each life some rain must fall.
Henry Wadsworth Longfellow

A riel the archangel was alive and well and keeping watch over our garden. How did I know this?

A certain species had taken over, that's how. And Ariel, the patron angel of wild animals, was protecting them.

We were once again the innocent victims of wild rabbits.

It was understandable when we lived at the Blue House, next door to a huge forest. But we were on the edge of a big city now, for heaven's sake!

Where did these wild rabbits come from? Did they follow us all this way? Was it retribution for the fox pee that we once poured around the garden beds to scare them off?

We had been more determined than ever to cooperate with wild things.

So we sympathized when the rabbits ate the stalks of the Annabelle hydrangea, leaving only a few twigs peeking above the ground. The winter was harsh, and wild animals had to survive, after all. And we knew that most of these hydrangea shrubs would send out new growth.

We sympathized when they ate the shoots of the evergreen euonymus that were leaning onto the verandah. The rabbits stripped them bare of every green leaf.

But we had to draw the line somewhere. We simply couldn't sympathize when they ate the bark off our young burning bush shrubs. This winter past, they stripped every single stalk of its protective covering.

In the back of my mind was a recent garden tragedy — the winter the rabbits stripped the lower branches and trunk of a tall, spreading burning bush that had stood by the driveway of the farmhouse for decades. It was a particularly glorious sight in the autumn, its leaves tinged with yellow, turning to red.

Stripped of its protective bark that winter, this beautiful plant, which had survived many winter storms and scorching droughts, withered and died.

Killed by furry little creatures. Like a giant Goliath, felled by the animal kingdom's version of tiny furry Davids with big ears, fluffy tails, and limpid eyes.

The rabbit problem caused a quandary of ethical proportions in our family.

Daughter Lauren felt protective. Already, she and her father had engaged in at least three heated arguments.

"They have a right to live, too!" I could hear her raised voice from the next room.

"And I'm all for that, but not in my garden!" her father replied, trying to keep his voice reasonably calm.

Meanwhile, the scavengers became so at home on our land that sometimes I wondered if they were trying to get into the house.

One day a rabbit sat on the verandah, just outside the front door.

I couldn't believe it. "Come on in, why don't you?" I said.

The rabbit froze.

Rabbits have a way of sitting perfectly still when they glimpse a human or other potential predator. Scientists think it's caused by fear but I have a different explanation: rabbits think if they don't move a muscle, we won't see them.

But how can you miss a rabbit that has gotten very fat from eating all your shrubs?

With the rabbit still on the verandah, I quietly closed the door and went to find Julius Caesar, one of our daughter's two little dogs that visited us often. Then I opened the door again and pointed out the rabbit sitting there, still as a rock, right in front of him.

Julius ran in the opposite direction.

The rabbit loped off. Julius saw it, reoriented himself, and sped after it. But by now the rabbit had an enormous head start. Julius never got close to Fred.

Oh — did I not mention that daughter Lauren had given the rabbits names?

Fred and Penelope, if you please.

How she knew the difference — if she knew the difference — I had no idea. And that actually didn't matter. What mattered was that she had made them almost members of the family.

Lord, give me strength, I thought.

I pointed out that there seemed to be several Freds and Penelopes on our property. But she insisted there were only two. And she was fond of them.

But how could only two rabbits do so much damage to our garden? She didn't reply.

"Fred is nibbling grass very peacefully," she observed, an hour or so later. Indeed, Fred was. On the lawn, just outside my kitchen window, not a care in the world.

"No. That's not grass! That's my forget-me-not flowers!" I squealed.

"Oh." Daughter nodded as if this was most natural.

She is protective of animals. She is the family member who once rescued a tiny white dog, got his medical needs taken care of, and named him Dawson.

So now the little rabbit vagabonds were under the protection of both the archangel Ariel and our daughter Lauren. For all I knew, Mr. Julius might even have been in cahoots with them — why else would he always run in the opposite direction?

Hamlin and I were determined to get rid of the critters that spring before his vegetable garden was planted. He brought the humane trap out of the garage and stocked it with carrots, lettuce, and other stuff that Beatrix Potter, author of the Peter Rabbit books, claimed rabbits love.

This strategy worked. But only twice.

First, the trap caught a rabbit that had fallen in with a bad crowd, the wild ones. It was a white rabbit, once a pet, which some human owner had abandoned.

She walked straight into the humane trap and the door shut behind her while she ate her belly full and settled down for a snooze. My husband gave her to friends, Linda and Daryl, who quickly discovered that her belly was full of other things, too. Within days, she gave birth to several kits, likely fathered by that dastardly wild rabbit, Fred.

The humane trap worked again, early that summer. And this time it caught one of the wild rabbits. Hamlin and I were delighted. Victory was finally ours.

It was a pathetic victory. The rabbit clawed and scrambled inside the trap, trying to fight its way out. And on the other side of the steel bars, another rabbit sat, watching. Every so often, the rabbit outside gave an unearthly cry of sorrow. Luckily for us, Lauren wasn't around that day, but I was heartsick.

"Oh, Lord!" I wailed to Hamlin. "I can't stand to look at this. I can't stand to hear that cry. I read that wild rabbits mate forever. Maybe we should release the rabbit in the trap."

"What? They've damn near destroyed the vegetable garden already! We can't let it out!"

I had no answer to that logic.

Hamlin softened. "We'll take him to the nearby nature reserve and come back and catch the other one. Then they'll be together."

And that's what he did.

But no one had told our plan to the second rabbit. He or she now feared that trap and never went near it again. Nor did any other rabbits. No matter how much lettuce or how many carrots we put inside.

But while I worried, the remaining rabbit quickly found another mate and did what rabbits do.

Now we were suffering from a plague of wild rabbits, for the second time in our lives.

"Time to rent a fox," I told my husband, remembering our experience with rabbits and foxes at the Blue House. "Only a fox can deter the rabbits."

"So you want to bring even more wild animals into our garden?" asked my unsmiling husband, without stopping to realize that my suggestion made no sense. How would we rent a fox, anyway?

CHAPTER 19
Mama's Garden

A thing of beauty is a joy forever
Its loveliness increases, it will never
Pass into nothingness; but still will keep
A bower quiet for us, and a sleep
Full of sweet dreams, and health, and quiet breathing.

John Keats

One garden here at the old farmhouse is extra-special. Precious, even. It's behind the house, on the side that gets the most sun.

Every Mother's Day, I head out to this garden. I sit on the bench at the end of the path. And I look around.

Partly shaded by a large red maple, the garden has two dogwood trees, two large purple lilacs, a Japanese maple, and a forsythia shrub. The Japanese maple was stuck there "temporarily" but was somehow forgotten and has now outgrown its spot.

"One of these days, we'll have to move it," my husband and I say. But the longer we wait, the more arduous the task becomes, which makes me suspect that the tree is there for the long haul.

It's in the only garden bed that accommodates such a variety of plants: those that love woodland and shade, and those that love strong sun.

Hydrangea shrubs and tree peonies flourish here. Solomon's-seal; several kinds of ferns; the intriguingly shaped Jack-in-the-pulpit; the occasional trillium (Ontario's official flower); mayapples; and another woodland plant whose name I never learned.

Pink tulips come up every spring, as do daffodils, astilbe, bloodroot, and miniature hosta.

But the thing that causes me the greatest joy is the arrival of the Easter lilies of my childhood. Those crocuses, brought with us from our previous home, are the first flowers to bloom every year.

And every morning while they bloom, I eagerly head out to Mama's Garden to see them and feel almost the same excitement I felt when, at seven years of age, I first saw these flowers. And I remember Mama. And the first Mama's Garden: the one she tended when I was a small child.

Mama's Garden II has an entrance arbour.

Up and around its trellises grow clematis vines that flower in pink and red. The pink ones bear hundreds of double blooms, the red bear small flowers, no more than two dozen every summer.

Throughout the spring, a pink-flowering groundcover, lamium, borders one side of Mama's Garden, while blue forget-me-nots border the other. Recently, though, they've both strayed into the path.

Your garden would look better if I could weed the path regularly, I apologize to Mama.

And I can hear her saying, Ah, m'dear. It'll get done. Right now, there are more important things on your plate.

So I'm listening to my mother. After all, the garden is named for her.

It's a reminder of that first garden I called Mama's Garden, in the hills of Jamaica. The small treasure box of a garden that Mama tended, perhaps with a bit of help from the fairies.

It's also a tribute to Mama's great love of gardening. To her talent at arranging flowers. And to one of the many lessons she taught us: one is never too poor or too busy to grow a garden.

My mother died several years ago. And that's why, every Mother's Day, I head out to Mama's Garden, no matter what the weather is like, no matter how I'm feeling. I bring a sturdy mug of coffee, and I walk through the entrance arbour and down the short pathway, looking at the flowers around me.

I sit on the stone bench at the back of the garden for a talk with Mama.

"Thank you," I tell her.

There are so many things I need to thank her for. So I talk to her, and I say a prayer of gratitude, and sometimes the talk gets mixed in with the prayer and it feels like the beings I am talking to are one and the same, but I don't think either Mama or God would mind.

I give thanks.

For a mother who loved and tended her family before all else. For a mother who was never too busy or too poor to grow a garden. And for a mother who passed on those lessons to me.

CHAPTER 20
After the Rain

Give yourself a gift: the present moment.
Marcus Aurelius

The skies turned dark, more grey than black. The air became perfectly still. And then came the rain, in sheets and showers. Pouring down on dry grass, thirsty garden beds...and our verandah roof.

The water streamed down in front of the verandah. I sat back in the comfortable cedar bench our friend Jean had made for us years earlier, enjoying this moment from a safe perch of my own.

"I should grab my camera," I told myself. But I remained still.

Small branches of pale-green leaves swayed in the air. The red weigela flowers shimmered amid green leaves, showered by water, ruffled by wind.

Below them, large hosta leaves dipped, weighed down by raindrops, before rising again.

Dip, dip. Spring back.

Unless you were, like the nearby berry bush, laden with red currants... in which case: dip, dip. Fall forward.

The tall blue spruce tree stood majestic, appearing unmoved by the wind and showers. But the tree had taken on a soft look, its face gentled by the rain. There was light movement in its outermost branches. All birds had taken cover, tucking themselves into dry spaces between the branches. All except one, who spied opportunity.

The bird darted into the rain, tail feathers dark, wet and glistening.

One determined swoop and it landed on its target. Just this once, it had what it usually had to wait or compete for: a space at the feeder. It pecked at the seeds, content.

Peck, peck, peck.

From the verandah's eaves trough, powerful streams torrented into the garden bed below. The Annabelle hydrangea was taking a beating. Branches, gracefully upright a few minutes ago, parted with the wisdom of growing things when faced with the unstoppable power of water.

It became a meditation: I watched, unmoving, softly breathing in and out.

The water from the eaves trough narrowed. Long thin streams formed a transparent drape in the space between verandah posts. Five streams falling steadily on the earth.

Then four. Then, three. Then two, then one.

A memory floated into my mind now and I saw it clearly, as if the event was taking place right there in front of me. My daughter as a young child, standing in the back doorway of the first house we owned, eager to share something that had just happened.

She was wet. She wore a yellow raincoat and matching rain boots but no hat. She was so delighted, her wet face shone like the sun.

And I remembered the verse I wrote for her later:

"I kissed the rain," my daughter said
As raindrops glistened on her head
The beads of water on her face
That shone with such delighted grace

Smiling, I drifted back to the present.

The rush of water, the soft thud of raindrops, the splash-splash on leaves and flowers — all had stopped. As if a mighty switch was turned on, then off, the rain had come and gone.

Flowers glistened. Birds chirped and flew together towards a single spot -- the feeder. And I thought, as I watched them compete:

How smart that first bird was. The one that went before, wet tail-feathers and all.

And how remarkable water is. Liquid, transparent, powerful.

And as I sat on the bench on our verandah, giving thanks for it all – the rain, the trees, the shrubs, the flowers, the grass, the birds, and a space in which to sit, protected — the sun came out.

It appeared as quickly as the rain began, except there was no warning this time. Almost no space between.

Rain and Sun. Each doing its part to keep us all alive.

We humans depend on them so much we take them for granted. We give them names that begin with common letters. But Rain and Sun are Capital Gifts. Sacred Gifts.

CHAPTER 21
A Slow Wisdom

When the leaves fall, we suddenly see all kinds of things
that were hidden. One morning I woke up and looked
through the window, and there was our stream, rushing
and sparkling through the woods.

From My Journal

In what seemed like a whole other life, I had written many stories, most never published, most hidden away and forgotten. My husband, frightened by my decline, went searching. He thought that finding the stories and getting me to read even some of them, would remind me of the powerful, confident woman I was before the accident.

He found them, I read them, and I was astonished at what I had written. Almost all were about the homes and people I had loved since childhood. And – did I really write this stuff? It seemed almost poetic in parts. Or was that wishful thinking?

We passed some of the stories to close relatives and friends, who said they loved them. Some also went to a magazine editor, who published them. Most went to our longtime friend, Tim Knight (yes, the hauler of rocks), with a simple, though timid, request: could he help me turn them into a book?

Timid, because I was still not thinking coherently much of the time and often stuttered when I talked. Whoever took on the job of helping me would need to understand my limitations. Tim did. He was my friend. We had also worked together on many projects at CBC Television, and I knew him to be a brilliant writer and editor. But would he agree?

I wouldn't have blamed him if he refused. After all, he had already rescued me at a defining moment in my journalism career. Tim was the CBC TV News executive who recruited me from journalism school, impressed with my qualifications and interview.

Years would pass before I finally learned a crucial detail of that recruitment process.

When the selection was being made, my journalism professor argued against me, insisting that I "would return to Jamaica" after graduation, so someone else should be chosen instead. If he had asked, he would have learned that I had already become a Canadian citizen, but he hadn't asked. Luckily for me, however, Tim overruled him.

You could say that Tim, having rescued me once, didn't need to do it again.

But he agreed and became the first and most important editor to work on the book. He was also surprisingly patient.

I teased him later that he had no choice: patience was the first job requirement.

When A Good Home was published in May of 2013, it felt like a community achievement. I had written its chapters over more than twenty years, but professional editors, family and friends had helped mold it. Even my therapist and doctor – my rehabilitation specialist at the hospital – joined my support network, urging me on, then becoming excited when the book was published.

Then came the invitations to carry out something called "author appearances": book readings in front of an audience. It frightened me so much, I returned to bed for two days and refused to leave the house.

Once again, my family, therapist, and doctor urged and encouraged me. Then family and friends had to gently push me out the door, drive me to the events, and sometimes even hold me upright. But they did and I did.

I was getting my first taste of being an author. My books were selling well, and more invitations were coming in.

And then I fell ill.

A pain-filled fall and winter got worse as we headed toward spring: the few times I went out, I caught something.

Flu. Bronchitis. A cough that wouldn't end. Worn out and afraid of falling, I rarely went outside, even to the verandah. Resigned to spending late winter in bed, I tried to write my way back to sanity and health.

Spring came.

And then.

"You've relapsed," my specialist said bluntly during my hospital visit.

"Guilty," I replied, staring at the floor. "Sorry."

"Do NOT feel guilty," she said. "It was an awful winter. All my patients with complex injuries had a very tough time."

She looked me in the eyes. "But your immune system is also weak," she warned. "Be very careful this spring, Cynthia."

I listened. I promised. And I was.

And then.

Gardening season began.

From my garden journal:

If gardening helped keep me sane, it stands to reason that not being able to garden helped drive me crazy.

Not being able to touch the soil, dig in the earth, feel the roots of a spreading plant before I dug it up and separated it to make two.

Not being able to dig two new holes with my trusty shovel, scooping aside the earth to place each plant in its own space then patiently refilling the hole around it with soil before watering and tamping down.

Not being able to do these things was a madness all its own.

Day after day, Hamlin worked hard in the garden. I watched, feeling entirely useless.

One day, he left on an errand.

And then.

As I turned, I spied a large crop of tiny blue-flowering forget-me-not plants creeping into the lawn from a garden bed. The longer I watched, the more they seemed to encroach.

I know they bug Hamlin, and I know they're easy to dig with a trowel. And so I thought I'd help.

A small thing.

A good thing.

I could do this.

I grabbed the trowel and made my way towards the truant flowers. I crouched over the lawn and started digging. I felt immensely useful. When the back and leg pain intensified, I stretched myself out on the lawn, face down. I dug again, sneezing as dust flew up into my nose.

Then I spied a few dandelions nearby.

"Stop!" said my wiser self. But I was already crouched over them, trowel engaged, dirt flying into my face and on my clothes.

I meant to stop. In just a few seconds. But my sense of time did not kick in. It rarely does.

And then.

When I got up, the pain almost knocked me out. I staggered. Stumbled. Fought against falling, my cane desperately trying to find purchase in the ground.

"Cynthia! Cynthia!" came the panicked shout. I had not heard my husband return.

I ask you: which is worse?

To watch your partner struggle with the gardening duties that you loved doing — on top of everything else that landed on his plate? Or risk even worse pain — and his distress — by doing a few small gardening things to help?

Some days, I'm almost used to the pain. It's with me all the bloody time.

But the guilt? I never get used to the guilt of watching him do all the gardening work.

It drives me nuts.

"Why do you do this?" He shook his head, frustrated and angry. "You know better!"

Yes I do.

So I'm obeying the doctor. Again. Sparing my husband distress. Again. Trying to cope with guilt. Again.

CHAPTER 22
It's Yellow with Petals

Let us be grateful for the people who make us happy;
they are the charming gardeners who make our souls
blossom.

Marcel Proust

I had to let go and allow others to do what I couldn't any more
As my role in the garden changed, so did Hamlin's. The man who once valued only vegetables and herbs ("Can you eat flowers?") had to learn about flowers.

I'm not saying he knew their names. He sometimes mangled them badly — especially the Latin ones like lobelia, liatris, and salvia.

When that happened, he resorted to describing them in unfathomable ways.

"You know ... the yellowish one ... no, it's kinda cream ... no, it's a kinda yellow with all those petals ..."

Kinda yellow with all those petals? I didn't want to embarrass him, so I racked my scrambled brain, trying to figure out which of several flowers he could possibly mean. Truth was, I had forgotten some of their names, but I still remembered more than he would likely ever know.

I walked him around what was now our flower garden. I tried to impart the differences between all the flowers with yellow petals: evening primrose, ligularia, several kinds of daisies, rudbeckia.

I knew he wouldn't remember the names, but I pointed and said them anyway. I told him which plants like sun, which like shade, and which ones thrive in some of each. The fact is, he had come a long way in a short time.I had come a long way, too. I learned to give him gardening advice and direction without feeling awkward about it. And I learned not to become impatient just because I know more about flowers than he does.

I now accepted and even appreciated some things that, once upon a time, would have driven me crazy.

As a young gardener, when caterpillars — future butterflies — fed on my flowering viburnum, I doused them with insecticide.

Now I let them be. Butterflies, bees, and other insects were too precious to spray away just because I wanted a neat and tidy garden.

I also knew that while gardening may seem to be a solitary vice, it really isn't. Gardeners learn from other gardeners. We swap plants, knowledge, and tomorrow's weather forecast.

And when we least expect it and need it most, a fellow gardener will get down on hands and knees and do the weeding. Once in a while, what goes around comes around.

One spring, long before the accident, an elderly couple's garden was so overgrown that they considered selling the property.

I volunteered to help out, and by late summer, the garden was tamed. The couple – Marion and Henry -- decided that, come the next spring, they'd be able to handle the gardening by themselves.

As their hearts lightened, our friendship deepened.

Then, years later, after the accident, Hamlin and I became the ones needing help.

Hamlin was working full-time running our company, serving on various charities, and taking care of our household.

I worried that tending the flower garden as well was too much to ask of him. "Maybe we should move," I kept saying.

But Hamlin wouldn't budge.

One day, my friend Kamala-Jean drove up from her home in downtown Toronto, looked around the garden, and declared, "I've come to weed!"

I was shocked, then embarrassed. How could I allow this elegant, accomplished woman — a leader in the community — to get down on her hands and knees in the soil of my garden beds?

Turns out I was wrong. Years earlier she'd sold her house and garden and moved into a condo on the waterfront. And she desperately missed her garden.

"I'm a gardener," she explained simply.

And so my friend visited two or three times a month in the gardening season, and while she weeded, I prepared a light lunch. Jamaican patties or slices of smoked salmon, always with a fresh salad from the garden.

And then we'd sit on the verandah and talk. About her grandchildren. About my children. About gardens and life.

Hamlin and I also got help from an expert. Rob, a master gardener, arrived every spring and autumn to help with some of the heavier, more complex tasks. He dug and planted the new flower-beds, including Mama's Garden. He trimmed the long cedar hedge, pruned the flowering shrubs.

My brother, Michael, sometimes worked with Hamlin to clean up the garden beds and lawn in spring.

Daughter Nikisha and her husband, Tim, had moved to new jobs in the United States, but daughter Lauren lived in Toronto and visited some weekends. During the gardening season, she helped by staining arbours and fences, picking up leaves, and doing other gardening chores. She had a busy career, so we especially appreciated her help.

Of course, wherever Lauren walked, eight little paws pattered along behind her. She occasionally stopped to play with her two little dogs: scratch under a chin or throw a ball.

Julius Caesar – the tiny dog with the big name – was five years old and frisky. Dawson was of indeterminate age – Lauren rescued him from abandonment a few years earlier, and the vet couldn't figure out his exact age, but noted that he was "getting on up there."

Lauren threw the ball and Julius sped towards it, retrieving it in no time flat. His half-Pug, half-Chihuahua body was comical: his trunk seemed to stay put while his four legs moved in different directions.

Dawson, meanwhile, ran gleefully in the opposite direction, tail wagging, ears flapping in the breeze. He stopped, searched for a moment, found nothing, but returned to Lauren in triumph. Maybe, at his age, just to run that far was a triumph.

Lauren laughed. I laughed. Both dogs seemed to laugh. And just like that, my spirits lifted, my worries lessened.

CHAPTER 23
The Trouble With Gardeners

If the sun dares to shine in January, the gardener is on tenterhooks lest the bushes will burst into bud too soon. If it rains, he fears for his little Alpine flowers; if it is dry, he thinks with pain of his rhododendrons and andromedas.

Karel Capek, The Gardener's Year

What is better on a winter day, when the garden is sound asleep and all of the north is covered with snow — what is better for a gardener than getting lost in a gardening book?

If, like most Canadians, you can't afford a winter home in the warm south, allowing you to comfortably tend your plants in what we northerners call 'the dead of winter,' what could be better?

And if, like almost all of humanity, you lack the funds to acquire a splendid, capacious, heated conservatory or 'orangerie', as some elegant people call fancy greenhouses — what is a gardener to do?

Well, you grab a blanket, curl up in a comfy chair or sofa — or on the floor, if you prefer — and read a book about the trials and tribulations of other gardeners.

Not just any book, of course. It must be witty. And not just any trials and tribulations – they must be comical. After all, it's already gloomy outside; why on earth would you read something even gloomier?

Author Beverley Nichols has long expired, but his gardening books are still alive and thriving. Two of them, Merry Hall and Down the Garden Path, can be relied on to make me laugh out loud.

How could I not enjoy an author who wrote as Nichols did in Merry Hall:

> *"Long experience has taught me that people who do not like geraniums have something morally unsound about them. Sooner or later you will find them out; you will discover that they drink, or steal books, or speak sharply to cats. Never trust a man or a woman who is not passionately devoted to geraniums."*

I love his writing, even though Nichols would not have liked me at all. Truth is, I once stole two books — from a convent, of all places. I had gone there for a silent retreat. My theft was inadvertent, and I confessed my crime to the nuns and returned the books — but only after I had read them both.

Worse than stealing books, I'm undevoted to geraniums, though I like them well enough.

This is partly because geraniums don't survive the Canadian winter outdoors. But it's mainly because other flowers stole my affections — peonies, poppies, and hydrangea. They are as charming and blousy as geraniums, and they're perennial. I am fond of hardy plants that come up from the soil on their own every year and pretty much take care of themselves.

But I'm devoted to Merry Hall, a book that's partly about Nichols' Georgian manor, but mostly about the formidable garden which he and his ancient gardener Oldfield tended together.

Well, not exactly together. Oldfield came with the garden, you see, and throughout the book, considers it his. Nichols, in his view, is merely the new arrival, from the city, a person who doesn't know anything about anything.

And Oldfield is partly right. For one thing, his regional accent is so strong, Nichols doesn't understand him most of the time. In Oldfield's way of talking, 'doves' become 'doovs' and 'a pond for ducks' becomes 'a pond for dooks.'

> *"Then dooks was chased away by Pomeranians," he continued.*
> *"I had a momentary vision of quantities of elderly gentlemen in coronets fleeing wildly across the lawn, clutching towels round their waists..."*

These two gardener-characters are a match made in reader heaven.

Give me, in the dead of winter, the older gardening books, the ones w
decades ago by gardeners who survived their own horticultural excesses
decided to tell the tale.

Utter ignorance combined with foolhardy optimism? Obsession bordering
on mania? We gardeners recognize ourselves immediately in such books.

Gardens may bring out the best in us, but we have a sneaky feeling that they
also reveal our madness.

We find ourselves cursing loudly at a weed, begging a prized plant to perk
up when we know it's already dead, or fervently digging something out of the
ground, unconcerned that our lovely behinds are sticking up in the air in full
view of passersby.

Czech author Karel Capek knew that, and that's why I love The Gardener's
Year.

> "I will tell you now how to recognize a real gardener. 'You must
> come to see me,' he says; 'I will show you my garden.' Then, when you
> go just to please him, you will find him with his rump sticking up
> somewhere among the perennials."

Yes, indeed. In our heart of hearts, many gardeners know the truth: we are
guilty of absurdity.

We keep buying plants when there's no room left to put them.

We pray for rain then complain that it prevents us from "getting out into the
garden."

We wash off the dirt, dress up, and attend a swanky dinner party only to
find ourselves passionately debating which is better – sheep or cow manure.

The Gardener's Year, is, in part, a homage to just that – manure. Capek
writes a lot about it, and one senses a twinkle of laughter in his eyes as he wrote:

> "A cartload of manure is most beautiful when it is brought on a
> frosty day, so that it steams like a sacrificial altar. When its fragrance
> reaches heaven, He who understands all things sniffs and says: 'Um,
> that's some nice manure.'"

Both Capek and Nichols wrote their gardening books after producing more
sombre work. Capek had written philosophical plays and books about human frailties,
and later, in the 1930's, he would write about the Nazi threat to Czechoslovakia.
Nichols had worked in Britain's military intelligence during the Second World War.

I imagine that between tackling such grim subjects, these writers needed to laugh. Because when I first read their books, I found useful gardening information, yes. But I sensed that they were having a laugh at themselves and all people who are silly enough to think we can control a garden.

And so their books take a comic view of the absurd behaviours that only a garden can evoke in the people who are foolish enough to tend them.

And that, perhaps, best explains why, despite all of Capek's and Nichols' serious writing, it's their gardening books that are most famous decades after they were first published.

Gardeners like me keep recommending them to friends who need some light reading during Canada's least humorous months – otherwise known as January, February, and March. Then each friend calls me, reads aloud a favourite excerpt, and laughs.

Capek and Nichols, two men both wise and foolish. Two men who gardened and loved it all: the cultivation, the frustration, the celebration. They made mountains out of molehills and rejoiced at tiny triumphs only a gardener could appreciate.

And despite their trials and tribulations, despite their own absurd actions (or perhaps because of them), they wrote rich, funny and revealing stories that, many years later, allow passionate gardeners to recognize themselves and laugh.

CHAPTER 24
Hamlin's Tender Care – for Daffodils

...When all at once I saw a crowd,
A host, of golden daffodils

William Wordsworth

I f you live long enough, you see the strangest things.

Dear reader, do you remember that first garden my husband and I planted?

Do you recall how I dragged Hamlin out of our house just after six o'clock one spring morning to see the tiny green tulip leaves popping up above the soil?

And do you remember that he shrugged? Yes, the man shrugged, entirely unimpressed by this miracle of birth.

His reaction was the first sign — though I didn't know it at the time — that he and I saw gardening in entirely different ways. He thought that only edibles, stuff you can eat like vegetables and herbs, were worth growing. I, on the other hand, loved flowers. Stuff that delights both the eye and the nose.

And thus began our first major disagreement. It took a fair bit of cooling down and negotiating to get over that particular marital dispute.

Now, decades later, we're living at the old farmhouse and Hamlin has developed a thing for daffodils.

Seriously — daffodils. Narcissus. And I'm flummoxed. Befuddled. Gobsmacked as my friend would say. Bouleversée as the French say.

Daffodils!

You may be wondering — is this the same man who's shared my life and my bed all these years?

Hamlin's newfound love started — strangely enough — while he was stuck in traffic. Driving up the Don Valley Parkway in Toronto, in one of those long-drawn-out moments of rush hour when the parkway turns into a parking lot, he glanced to his left and experienced a Wordsworthian moment.

You may recall that verse from the Wordsworth poem. The one you had to memorize at school for the test:

> *I wandered lonely as a cloud*
> *That floats on high o'er vales and hills*
> *When all at once I saw a crowd,*
> *A host, of golden daffodils;*
> *Beside the lake, beneath the trees,*
> *Fluttering and dancing in the breeze.*

There was no lake for Hamlin. But the parkway runs through a beautiful valley. And so there were hills and vales and trees. And in the near distance, a stream of golden daffodils did indeed flutter and dance in the spring breeze.

And in that moment, my husband fell in love.

With daffodils.

It was the daffodils that caused Hamlin to reorganize his priorities that fall.

He claimed that he simply didn't have enough time to do all his usual gardening tasks. Like removing the hundred-year-old evergreens that were well past their best-before date. And trimming the cedar hedges that had grown too tall. Then there were the shrubs that needed pruning, or transplanting. And all that cleaning up around the garden beds…

"I can't do everything," he complained. "Some things just won't get done this fall."

I sympathized. And felt guilty for the umpteenth time because my body still hadn't healed, and I couldn't help him.

Then, even though he was so burdened with tasks, Hamlin went out and bought several big bags full of bulbs.

"They're daffodils," he explained as he carried the bags into the house.

He went to the kitchen window. "Where should I plant them?" He eyed the back lawn. "Seems daffodils need space."

I tried to hide my surprise. "Oh … under the apple trees. I read somewhere that daffodils do well under apple trees. Plus, the trees are on a slope and it gets reasonably good sun."

"Hmm …"

A little later I glanced out the kitchen window, and there he was, out in the back garden, digging up clumps of lawn and burying bulbs under and around our two ancient apple trees.

Hundreds and hundreds of daffodil bulbs.

Hamlin dug, placed, tamped, watered, put the lawn clumps back in place, and hours later walked back into the house, tired but immensely pleased with himself.

There were days, as the winter wore on long past its due departure date, when I would catch him staring out the back window, eyeing the deep blanket of snow covering his daffodil bulbs.

"Think my daffodils will make it?" he asked, not bothering to disguise the anxiety in his voice.

"Sure, they will!" I promised.

This exchange reminded me of the first autumn we dug a trench and buried our fig tree in the garden soil. We worried that this Mediterranean fruit tree couldn't possibly survive a long Canadian winter. But, insulated by the soil, the fig tree survived. And so would Hamlin's daffodils.

"They will make it," I repeated.

I read the look on his face and hugged him.

When the snow on the garden finally started to melt, Hamlin's worries resurfaced. He stood at the same window and pointed out that the snow covering the daffodil bulbs wasn't melting as fast as everywhere else.

"I'm thinking of removing the snow myself," he said.

I laughed. Then I realized he wasn't joking. He was actually thinking of removing a small mountain of snow. To save his daffodils. The plants you can't eat.

The next day he put on his old gardening clothes and Wellingtons for the first time since fall and headed out into the garden. He stood between the two big old apple trees for a long time, peering down at the snow.

I watched him stand there and felt oddly relieved that there was no snow shovel in his hand. He finally turned around and walked back to the house.

"I'm a bit worried about my daffodils under the snow."

"Just wait. Your daffodils will bloom. Give them time."

But I was also thinking, If you live long enough, you see the strangest things.

My husband agonizing over whether his daffodils will survive the snow, sprout, and bloom?

His daffodils?

I hugged him again.

CHAPTER 25
The Garden Party

Everybody needs beauty as well as bread
Places to play in and pray in
Where nature may heal and give strength to body and
soul.

John Muir Naturalist

H amlin and I padded out to the verandah in our comfortable slippers, pyjamas clearly visible under our bathrobes, and coffee mugs in hand.

It was June, and this simple early-morning activity had become a ritual of spring.

We sat in the wooden Muskoka chairs, silently gazing at the garden as we sipped. The air was fresh and clean, the nearby lawn damp with dew.

Occasionally, we looked at each other and smiled, feeling no need to break the silence. Even the morning chorus of our feathered friends had quieted.

Peace.

My eyes took in the different shapes. The vine-covered arbours, the trees, the wooden benches. The curving boxwood hedge that bordered several garden beds, neatly clipped by Hamlin only a week before.

And there was sunshine. Still gentle at this time of morning, it was a welcome sign of good weather to come.

I glanced at my beloved and we both smiled again, no doubt sharing the same thought: it's a perfect day for a garden party.

Today we were going to do something I had long hoped for. Our friends from the early Sunday morning service at our church would be joining us for afternoon tea on Ambercroft's large verandah and in the garden.

Every spring, I had dreamed of this. To plan, organize, and host an afternoon tea party in the garden. And every year, Hamlin helped me face the reality: I wasn't well enough.

But this year was different. I convinced him that I would write out a good plan, ask for help, and start preparations a few days before. I also promised that I would not "overdo it." Hamlin agreed. We set the date.

I sent the invitations. "Come to afternoon tea," I wrote. "On the verandah and in the garden."

Nearly a dozen friends accepted. Pleased with their responses, I followed that with a piece of brash foolishness.

"I'm doing it all myself," I proudly told Hamlin.

Silence.

By myself, I had rarely entertained more than one person at a time, afraid that I wouldn't be able to handle it. The head injury meant that complex arrangements were a huge challenge. The constant pain and PTSD nightmares meant that some days I could hardly get out of bed by myself.

"Okay," he finally said. I couldn't tell what he was thinking.

Carefully, I made a menu, then a shopping list, and then a detailed schedule. Nothing could be left to memory. I checked everything a million times.

The day before the event, we tidied the verandah, dusted off chairs and small tables and brought out brightly-coloured cushions. Then I prayed for good weather. And now here it was, the day I had dreamed of, sunshine and all. Visitors would arrive in the early afternoon.

"I can manage," I told Hamlin with great outward confidence and inner trepidation. "You can help me greet the guests and serve the drinks."

"Sure you have enough food?" he asked.

"I've got it all under control," I said. I couldn't tell if he was reassured.

I encouraged him to go for a ride with his cycling buddies that morning while I prepared.

At one end of our long and deep verandah, the table was covered with a white tablecloth — my old standby. The former chenille bedspread once belonged to my mother but I had pressed it into service as an outdoor tablecloth because it had two holes at one end. I had mastered the art of carefully tucking the damaged parts out of sight.

A vase with fresh-cut flowers stood in the centre of the table. Glasses, stacks of plates, napkins and cutlery were set out, along with pretty vintage cups and saucers. I planned to serve tea, cold drinks, a fruit salad and a variety of appetizers, hot and cold.

Hamlin phoned on his way home.

"Shall I pick up a couple quiches?"

"No," I said. "I have enough food."

"Hmmm…" he said.

The garden was glorious that day. The sun shone brightly, flowers bloomed, birds sang their welcome.

I heard the first car drive up, and I took a deep breath. Our guests were starting to arrive.

Hamlin smoothly took over: the greetings, the drinks, the house and garden tours.

In the kitchen, I smelled something delicious.

Quiches warming in the oven.

Thank you, my beloved.

Muriel, an acclaimed artist, walked down the hallway beside her husband Michael. Hamlin and I waited, smiling. She stopped suddenly and stared at two paintings on the wall.

"Oh, goodness!" she exclaimed, eyes sparkling. She touched Michael's arm. "Oh, look at this!"

The paintings had been recent gifts from Muriel. The smaller painting depicted a floral arrangement Muriel had been given. The larger painting showed a patch of red poppies blowing in the wind.

Muriel had decided to discard the larger painting because the wind had been working against her that day and she felt the painting looked wild, the poppies askew. But we loved it, and she handed it over to us.

Just days before the tea party, Hamlin had them framed and hung on the wall where he knew Muriel would see them. He had planned this surprise well.

We beamed at her now as she declared: "Oh! But it looks much better framed! I had no idea."

"Want it back?" I asked, smiling mischievously and reaching to hug her. She hugged back.

Hamlin continued the tour. I lingered to watch Muriel and Michael discover the interior of our house, making appreciative murmurs as they went along. Though Muriel, Michael and I chatted by phone at least once a week, this was their first time visiting.

For a moment, I saw the house through their eyes, the eyes of newcomers.

To say Ambercroft looked beautiful didn't quite describe it. Inside, the house seemed to possess a new elegance, grace, and warmth.

Outside, the garden shone with a dazzling radiance.

An abundance of deep pink peonies, clouds of blue forget-me-nots, cream-and-yellow irises, all set off by the green leaves of shrubs and trees towering overhead.

A blue-flowering clematis vine covered one whole side of the large arbour near the verandah. But it was the honeysuckle vine on the other side of the arbour that stole the show. The citrus-y fragrance of its cream-coloured flowers wafted towards us on the slightest breeze.

Our guests ooed and aahed as butterflies, bees, and birds floated by. A male cardinal had perched on the arbour, undeterred by the humans watching him nearby. His brilliant red feathers glowed against the white wood of the arbour and the green of the clematis leaves that covered it.

Gundy, one of our guests, had her camera handy. She took several photos of the gardens, the bird, and our other guests.

Good friends know. They know when you mean well but are struggling. It wasn't long before Joanne, Jane, Doreen and several others took charge, telling Hamlin and me to sit down, that they would help themselves. Then they served food and drink.

Ah, the blessing of good friends, I thought.

"Thanks for hosting us," I teased.

When the party ended, we held hands, as we do at church gatherings. Led by Reverend Claire, we said "the grace."

"May the grace of our Lord Jesus Christ, and the love of God and the fellowship of the Holy Spirit," she began. Each hand got a squeeze of friendship as we said the final words: "... be with us now and evermore. Amen."

CHAPTER 26
Sins and Virtues

Wisdom is oft-times nearer when we stoop than when we soar.

William Wordsworth

I have been a fierce and passionate gardener, living by the credo that anything worth doing is worth doing well — or at least till exhaustion takes over.

It's been an emotional journey, right from the first garden I grew as an adult to the one that surrounds our house today. And along the way, I confess, I've committed not only absurdity, but all of the Seven Deadly Sins.

Greed. Lust. Envy. Gluttony. Pride. Wrath. Sloth.

In my defence, I did not willingly commit the seventh, Sloth. At least, not in the spiritual sense. It was forced on me – brought on by injuries and pain from an accident.

But Sloth, in the sense of physical laziness, is a whole different matter. I even recommend it as part of one's relationship with the garden. Not all the time, mind you. But as a much-needed break from all that hard work. To really enjoy the garden, one must learn to stop - to laze a bit - and admire the fruit of one's labours.

Along with a new respect for slowing down and being lazy in the garden, I've found myself of necessity developing a kind of serenity about my garden. Serenity and a large dose of common sense. These two never made it into any version of the Seven Heavenly Virtues — at least, not explicitly — but they should have.

If I'd ever prayed for lots of time off work, I must have forgotten the fine print.

"Lots of time off work and good health to enjoy it" is what I should have prayed for. Instead, I've ended up with a big fat irony: I finally have all the time in the world to garden – and cannot do it.

But when I look back at the last several years, I'm surprised at how much I've gained from simply having a place where flowers grow.

There's so much more to gardening than digging, planting, and watering. It's the surplus my mother used to talk about, except she called it by its Jamaican name — brawta — or its English name — grace.

Grace. The unexpected gift, over and above what you paid for, more than you ever expected. The thing you can't earn, plead, or bargain your way into.

I'm the beneficiary of grace in many aspects of my life. God's grace. The grace of my family's love. The grace of friendship. The grace of nature. Of my garden. And the grace of caring individuals who tend it for me.

There is grace in our gardens. Like plants that thrived when the odds were heavy against them.

For instance, over the years I'd been frustrated by the wisteria that refused to bloom. Then one day as I grumbled my way to the back of the garden, I caught a glimpse of something lavender-mauve.

Wisteria blooms. Long panicles of gorgeous, fragrant, purple wisteria blooms, brilliant among the green leaves.

This was the same tiny sucker, now grown up, that Hamlin had brought from the Blue House garden. You may remember his proclamation at the time that it had roughly the same chance of survival as a snowball in hell.

For years, while we fussed over the bloomless mature wisteria in the front garden of the farmhouse, this little vine sat in its forsaken spot, gathering strength to put on a splendid first show.

It has bloomed every spring since then.

Then there was the rose of Sharon. A late spring transplant from a neighbour's garden, it had lain out in the hot sun, bare roots and all, for days before planting.

We planted, we watered, but over the summer, it languished, as if unsure whether to live or die. Not a bloom in sight.

And then on a warm day in mid-October it came alive. It bloomed and bloomed and bloomed, sending out lovely pink flowers — the last flowers in the garden before the snows came and turned everything brown.

Someone once asked if I believe in miracles.

"Of course there are miracles," I replied. "Have you never walked in a garden in spring?"

A person should never hurry through a garden. You have to learn to stop and look. And, oh, what marvellous things you'll see! That rhododendron, the one you thought the harsh winter had killed, is sending out a new leaf. That hint of green under the needles of the pine tree — tiny shoots of blue-flowering scilla, braving the cold. Gardens remind us to be mindful of miracles.

Just when you think a plant is dead, it pops through the earth. Or sends out green leaves. Just when you think a vine will never bloom, it showers you with panicles of fragrant purple flowers. Gardens remind us to hope.

We can't hurry a flower or a tree, although I've often wished I could. Seasoned gardeners know that it takes the time it takes. Gardens remind us to be patient.

I could never walk through my garden without stopping to weed, or deadhead the roses and day lilies. Now that I've accepted my mandatory slow-down (my Sloth), I find myself simply looking, learning, and enjoying the garden more. I still get frustrated at times, but much less so now. And I'm enjoying planting again — in containers on my verandah. Gardens remind us to accept.

When I was a child, I thought the fairies were the ones who brought the tiny crocuses that bloomed every Easter in my mother's tiny garden in the Jamaican countryside. One day they weren't there (or so I thought), but the next, there they were, blooming in all their miniature glory.

Pain, worry, and outright fear can take away a person's sense of wonder, but there's nothing like a garden in spring or summer to bring it back. The shimmer of raindrops on round green leaves. The mysterious waltzing movement of a tall fern when there's no breeze. The unexpected bloom of a woodland phlox beneath bigger plants. Gardens will, if you let them, restore a childlike wonder to a wearied soul.

There is such joy in a garden. The joy of discovery. The joy of watching a transplant find its strength in a new place. The joy of seeing a flower bloom. The joy of fragrant roses. Gardens remind us of the true meaning of enjoyment.

To enjoy the garden — its lessons, its miracles, its healing powers — one should not stomp through it, always trying to control and fix.

One must allow time and space for the soul of the garden – the garden's shape and flow and colour – to unfold. The unexpected gifts — from the bees, the air, the birds. The flowers and berries that we didn't plant, blooming with a kind of joy. These and other dollops of grace, these and other joyful surprises. Gardens can teach us about grace.

Gardens can also comfort. As they have done for me.

And this, above all: Gardens can help us to accept love and to love more deeply than we thought possible.

I have watched my husband's love expand till I thought he couldn't do any more. I saw it in the flowers he transplanted, the bulbs he planted, the arbours he built. I have learned to accept the love and contributions of family and friends without feeling overly guilty — and to find new ways to express my own gratitude and love.

And through it all, I have learned that there is no limit to love. That it is possible for love to grow even more deeply and meaningfully than one ever thought was possible.

The End

Author Bio

CYNTHIA REYES, author of *A Good Home*, *An Honest House* and the children's books *Myrtle the Purple Turtle*, *Myrtle's Game* and *Myrtle Makes a New Friend*, returns to the gardens she loves with *Twigs in My Hair – A Gardening Memoir*.

A former television journalist, trainer and executive producer with the Canadian Broadcasting Corporation, Cynthia has also written feature stories for Arabella Magazine, The Toronto Star, The Globe and Mail and other publications.

Awards and recognition include the Trailblazer Award, the CBC President's Award, the Children's Broadcast Institute Award, the Crystal Award for Outstanding Achievement in Film and Television, and the Diamond Award for Book of the Year. In 2016, she was inducted into the Order of Distinction – Commander Level, by Jamaica, her country of birth. Cynthia and her husband live in a small town in Ontario, Canada.

Garden Photos

The photos in this book are provided by Hamlin Grange.

He complains that he didn't know they would have been used for a book, or he would have done better! But I love his photos, and I wanted to show you images of some of our gardens; he kindly agreed to show them in this book.

I have no pictures of my childhood gardens – Jamaican farm families didn't often stop to take pictures back in those days. I also have none of the first gardens Hamlin and I created in Toronto. We were too busy arguing, or trying to figure out what we were doing!

Instead, we share selected photos from our later gardens. We hope you enjoy them.

Acknowledgements

You've read this book, so you know I could not have done it alone.

Thanks, first of all, to Hamlin Grange, who provided the photos for this book, and many of the anecdotes, too! He claims his sole purpose in life is to be a source of amusement for my readers, but we all know that's not true.

Thanks to our mothers, whose love for gardening has provided sustenance for our family through food, encouragement, and wisdom over the years.

Thanks to our daughters Nikisha Reyes-Grange and Lauren Reyes-Grange, my sons-in-law Tim McCarthy and Dan Leca and my siblings, Yvonne, Pat, Jaqui and Michael, all beloved and appreciated.

Deep bows to my editors, Tim Knight and Don Bastian, and my writing mentor, Lesley Marcovich: you have been faithful partners through the years.

Thanks to educator and gardener Arna Sloan who read and proofread the first version of this book, and to author-editor-bookstore owner Jennifer Bogart, final proofreader.

Beta readers are a blessing to all of my books. They provide valuable feedback on various drafts of the manuscript. Thanks to Carol Shaw, Gail Scala, Linda Similas and Nory Siberry.

The back-cover reviews come from three authors who are expert gardeners: Jean Gairdner, Dr. Hilary Custance Green and Sheryl Normandeau. Thank you all for reading and reviewing.

Les Lawrence, artist and gardener, is also the "Les" of the chapter titled A Bloomin' Competition. He was the perfect artist to create the black and white illustrations. Thank you, Les.

Clif Graves, book designer, claims he doesn't know flowers, but bravely agreed to design a gardening memoir anyway. Thanks for warmly welcoming this experience, Clif!

My circle of support includes friends at St. Thomas' Anglican in Brooklin, Ontario, and members of BOAA in Bowmanville, Ontario. It includes readers of my books, blog, and magazine articles and many followers on Facebook and Twitter. And it includes librarians and teachers, many of whom I have never met in person.

Finally, I give thanks for the grace of God, the bounty of Nature, and the good that comes from Love.

Twigs in My Hair

Praise for *A Good Home*

Colin McAllister and Justin Ryan, Colin and Justin TV:
"When Cynthia Reyes dips her pen in ink (for this is how we imagine her, immersed in traditional techniques and devoid of modern day conveniences like laptop or iPad) she creates magic; captivating, heavenly prose falls from her quill. She's indeed a gifted scribe and, leafing the pages of *A Good Home* (gripped, as we were, from the opening paragraphs) we hung on her every, emotive word."

Andrea Stephenson, Writer and Blogger
"Warm and moving, there are touches of grace everywhere in this memoir. It is a story of family, community, love and a life well lived. A story of generations of strong women and the life experiences that made them. This is a book that feels magical, as though for a while you've stepped into another world that is sure to move you and teach you some important life lessons on the way. I didn't want to stop reading, but fortunately the sequel, *An Honest House*, has just been published, so I didn't have to!"

Susan Marjetti, Canadian Broadcasting Corporation:
"Read 14 books this summer. Most memorable? *A Good Home*, by Toronto's Cynthia Reyes. An enriching and lasting experience."

Praise for *An Honest House*

Andrea Torrey, author of *The Great & the Small*
"Cynthia's way of telling a story of her life's ever-changing landscape is so gentle, almost like the changing of the seasons that nature undergoes with grace and dignity, without resistance. Her observations of the small moments that make up happiness caused me to ponder the small moments that make up my own. She is a philosopher of the everyday joy of what it means to be alive."

Diane Taylor, author of *The Gift of Memoir*:
"Good memoirs bring light into the world, and *An Honest House* beams light from every page… I highly recommend immersing yourself in *An Honest House*."

Cynthia Jobin, author of *Song of Paper*
"This elegant memoir is beautifully written, full of heart, humor and joy in the ordinary days and things of life. It is a work of fresh air and light; it will leave you not only hoping, but believing that life is good. Did I say humor? There's plenty of that, too, and it's a delight!"

CPSIA information can be obtained
at www.ICGtesting.com
Printed in the USA
LVHW071616311019
635968LV00018B/1392/P

9 780991 837922